Buying and Running Your Own Business

Buying and Running
Your Own Business

IAN FORD

London

BUSINESS BOOKS LIMITED

SBN 220 66868 X

*This book has been set in 10 on 12 pt Times New Roman
by William Clowes and Sons, Limited, London and Beccles
for the publishers, Business Books Limited
(registered office: 180 Fleet Street, London, E.C.4)
publishing offices: Mercury House, Waterloo, London, S.E.1*

MADE AND PRINTED IN GREAT BRITAIN

Contents

Introduction

More people than ever before are contemplating leaving their wage or salaried employment to seek independence and security by buying their own business. There are many reasons for this, but undoubtedly the main one arises from the difficult national economic conditions which are prevailing.

Companies are becoming very conscious of the savings which can be made by reducing their labour force, at the same time taking full advantage of the capital grants and other incentives available under the many Government schemes in operation to encourage this trend. Modern plant and machinery is being installed to reduce the number of operatives required on the factory floor to cut production costs. Computers and other accounting machines are being introduced to reduce office staff and thus save overhead expenses. There have also been many reports in the national press of large numbers of people made redundant arising from mergers of large companies or the closure of factories.

In this mass production age, another reason is that machines are daily reducing the demand for work requiring trade skills and substituting semi-skilled work which can be uninteresting and give little, if any, job satisfaction. Until comparatively recent times it was reluctantly accepted during periods of trade recession that the factory worker would be the main sufferer, as he stood a greater chance of being laid off than the white-collar worker; this is no longer true. Redundancy can equally apply to factory and office workers, senior executives and even at director level.

It is from all sections of the working population, therefore, that interest in buying a business is being shown.

From 1954 many families have been able to acquire capital and are now in a position to consider the idea seriously, especially if the receipt of a large sum in the form of redundancy pay is expected. Many people have the incentive and the means to acquire a business, therefore, but at the same time realize their savings could be severely depleted or lost by purchasing a money-losing business through lack of experience. These fears can be justified. At law, there is a maxim 'let the buyer beware'. This means the onus is on a buyer to satisfy himself properly that everything is in order, as he cannot expect to receive redress if, after buying, it transpires the purchase was not up to expectation. There are rare exceptions to this rule, the main ones being where at the time the buyer entered into the contract he was under a threat, or under the influence of drugs or alcohol, or in the case of fraudulent misrepresentation.

The purpose of this book is twofold. First, to make the reader aware of the pitfalls to be encountered in buying a business, at the same time showing him how they may be recognized if they exist; secondly, to give him a basic understanding of the problems involved.

When you find a business which appeals to you, you will be able to undertake a preliminary investigation and make the more elementary enquiries yourself and, if at the end you are still interested, you can then engage professional advice and compare it with your own opinion. You will appreciate that, without any knowledge of buying a business, you will rely very heavily on your accountant and solicitor and could incur considerable expense, only to be advised not to proceed because of some matter which came to light during their investigations. You will then go through the whole process again with possibly the same result.

It is the aim of this book to stop you saying at some future date after buying a business, 'What made me buy it in the first place? I was better off working for somebody else.' There are instances of a man and wife team losing their savings by buying a bad business where it subsequently transpired it was unsaleable. The ambitions and dreams can end up by closing down the business and the buyer only too happy to relet the premises and not able to recover a penny of his original capital investment in the process.

Having said that, you may be assured the majority of businesses available for purchase are satisfactory, as it is possible to make a comfortable living out of them, as many couples have discovered for themselves. They have also found that by running a business of their own, although sometimes involving them in longer working hours, they are relieved of many of the strains and tensions which sometimes accompany working for an employer.

Finally, always remember, when you have read this book, you will receive good advice from your accountant and solicitor, but in the end it must be your decision alone whether or not to purchase. Therefore, the more understanding you show in the problems involved, the better your final judgement will be.

Part one – Buying a Business

CHAPTER I

How to Trade

One of the first decisions you must make is the form under which you are going to trade. The choice is between a sole trader, partnership or limited company. If you propose to own the business yourself, then the choice is between a sole trader or limited company. If you have a business partner, for example your wife, then it must be either a partnership or limited company.

Sole Trader

This applies to an individual where the business is his sole property and he is trading on his own account. The main advantage of a sole trader is that he need not conform to any rules or regulations in his method of trading provided, of course, he trades in accordance with law. He is not accountable to anyone other than himself, he can make his own decisions and change his policies as often as and when he wishes. All the profits of the business are his; likewise he must suffer all losses.

The main disadvantage is in the event of insolvency, when the creditors of the business may look to the personal assets of the sole trader if they are not fully discharged out of the business. As an example, a sole trader is insolvent with business creditors of £4,000. The sole trader also owns a house in his own name valued at £5,000. The business is sold realizing £1,000. The creditors will be able to claim the £1,000 received for the business and will also have the right through the process of law to sell the house and receive a further £3,000 out of the proceeds to satisfy their own claims.

If a sole trader carries on his business in any name other than his own, he must inform the Registrar of Business Names, 55–71 City Road, London, E.C.1. accordingly. A small registration fee is payable.

Partnership

The Partnership Act, 1890 defines a partnership as being 'The relationship which subsists between persons carrying on a business in common with a view of profit'.

As more than one person is involved, it is advisable for them to formulate at the outset a set of business rules which they will then be obliged to conform to. The rules will be in the form of a Deed of Partnership, the important clauses of which should provide for:

1 How the profits and losses are to be divided between themselves: both trading profits and capital profits.
2 The amount of capital each partner must contribute to the business.
3 Partners' salaries (if any).
4 Arrangements for the preparation of proper annual accounts and for their audit.
5 Arrangements as to the drawings of the partners (if any).
6 The valuation of goodwill, especially in the event of retirement or death of one of the partners.
7 Arrangements as to the payment of interest on capital and loans (if any) and the charging of interest on drawings.
8 Arrangements for arbitration in the event of the partners failing to agree between themselves on the interpretation of any of the clauses in the Deed of Partnership.

It sometimes happens that partners commence business without any formal deed being entered into. In this event, and until such time as a Deed of Partnership is entered into, the rights and duties of the partners are established by the Partnership Act, 1890, the main provisions being:

1 Partners are entitled to share equally in the capital and trading profits and must contribute equally to losses, whether of a capital nature or otherwise.
2 Partners are entitled to receive out of the undertaking interest at the rate of 5 per cent per annum on any advances, i.e. loans, they may make in the business apart from capital.
3 Partners are not entitled to any salary for acting in the partnership business. (They will, of course, be entitled to their share of profits.)

4 Partners are not entitled to be credited with interest on the balances of their capital accounts prior to the ascertainment of profits.

As in the case of the sole trader, the partners are personally liable for the whole of the debts of the business even to the extent of their personal assets.

Again as in the case of a sole trader, if the business trades under a name other than the names of the partners, then the Registrar of Business Names must be notified to this effect.

Limited Company

There are three classes of limited companies namely:

1 Companies limited by guarantee.
2 Unlimited companies.
3 Companies limited by shares.

The first two classes (1) and (2) above need be of no concern to you and will not be referred to again. We only need concentrate on companies limited by shares, where the liability of its members is limited to the extent of the face value of the issued share capital of the company.

There are two classes of companies limited by shares, public companies (again of no further interest to this book) and private companies. A private company is defined as one which:

1 Restricts the right to transfer its shares.
2 Limits the number of its members to fifty (excluding present and ex-employees).
3 Prohibits any invitation to the public to subscribe for any of its shares or debentures.

As a limited company may sue and be sued at law in its own right, it is essential that persons or companies who may have dealings with it have the opportunity of seeing for themselves the rules which govern the running of the company, if they so wish. The rules are in two parts. In general terms, the first set of rules regulates the company's activities with third parties (known as the Memorandum of Association), and the second set governs the internal management of the company (Articles of Association).

The Memorandum of Association must state:

1 The name of the company with 'Limited' as the last word of the name.
2 The domicile of the company, i.e. whether the registered office of the company is to be situated in England (including for this purpose Wales) or Scotland.
3 The objects of the company, i.e. the purpose for which it is formed, and the powers taken to enable it to carry out that purpose.
4 That the liability of the members is limited.
5 The amount of share capital with which the company proposes to be registered and the division thereof into shares of a fixed amount.

The important one is the objects clause—see (3) above. This must state clearly the trade which the company proposes to undertake. It is also advisable to extend the clause to include trades which the company may diversify into at a later date. The reason for this may be shown by the following example. The objects clause only provides for a company to sell confectionery, newspapers and tobacco. The company prospers and it is decided to expand by investing the profits of the business in a shoe shop. Because the Memorandum does not permit this, the purchase of the shoe shop does not have the authority of the company and if the acquisition should fail, then the directors of the company may be held to be personally liable for the debts incurred.

The Articles of Association should include the following provisions in addition to the three clauses already referred to in defining a private company:

1 Rules for the issue of shares and for the variation of rights of the various classes of shareholders, i.e. ordinary, deferred and preference shareholders.
2 When and how calls are to be made on the members in respect of moneys unpaid on shares.
3 Rules covering the transfer of shares.
4 Rules covering the alteration of capital.
5 Provision for holding meetings of members, giving notice of such meetings, rights of members to vote and for regulating the proceedings of meetings.

6 The number of directors, and how they may be appointed or retired.

7 The powers and duties of directors (if they exceed these powers then they may be held personally liable in the event of loss), their remuneration, and whether or not they must hold shares in the company as a qualification for them to act as directors.

8 Rules covering the use of the seal. When directors sign a document which has been sealed, they are only signifying they witnessed the use of the seal.

9 Rules governing the declaration of dividends and the transfer of profits to reserves.

10 Rules governing the keeping of proper accounts and for their audit.

Before an English company has legal existence, the Registrar of Companies, 55–71 City Road, London, E.C.1. must issue a Certificate of Incorporation (the equivalent of a birth certificate). To obtain this certificate the following documents must be presented to the Registrar:

1 A copy of the Memorandum of Association.

2 A copy of the Articles of Association.

3 A declaration that all statutory requirements have been complied with in forming the company.

4 A statement of the authorized share capital of the company.

In the case of a company to be domiciled in Scotland, the same documents must be sent to the Registrar of Companies, Edinburgh.

There are two main sources available from which a limited company can be obtained. You can instruct your solicitor to form one for you, which unfortunately tends to be expensive, or purchase one through a ready-made company broker. The latter is the simplest and cheapest method. There are many firms advertising themselves in the national press, who form and sell companies just as a tobacconist buys and sells cigarettes. The company which you buy will not have traded before so there is no danger of acquiring liabilities with it. All you need do is to telephone the broker giving him the nature of business you propose to undertake, and you will receive a limited company together with its Certificate of Incorporation and necessary Statutory Books, etc. within 24 hours at a cost varying from £30 to £40. It sometimes happens, however, that you have a name for the company which does not appeal to you, in which event you can change the name at an additional cost of £10.

Alternatively, from the same source, you can order a company with a name of your own choosing, provided it is acceptable to the Registrar, and within 10 days the company will be incorporated. The cost will vary from £35 to £45, but again it will be less expensive than a solicitor will charge if he formed one for you.

There is no reason why a limited company should not trade under a name other than its own, for example through the name of the business it acquires, with the same proviso as hitherto of informing the Registrar of Business Names.

The final stage of this chapter must be to translate all this information into practical terms.

From the taxation point of view:

1 If you expect the business to make annual profits of up to £5,000 (at which stage surtax is payable on earned income), and it is the intention to take out of the business all the profits as income, then there is no advantage one way or the other between a sole trader/partnership, or limited company. Under these circumstances, a limited company is recommended.

2 If you expect the business to make annual profits of up to £5,000 and intend to retain as much of the profits in the business as possible for future expansion, then the advantage lies with the sole trader or partnership.

3 If the annual profits are to be in excess of £5,000, then it may be advantageous to have a limited company, but the advice of your accountant is recommended as it must depend on the anticipated level of profits and the income you propose to receive from the business.

Limited Companies: Other advantages
1 As your wealth is represented by shares in a limited company, it is easier to make gifts to avoid estate duty. All you need do is to give shares in the company to your relations or other prospective beneficiaries and provided you live for 7 years thereafter, no estate duty is payable on the gift. (There is a reducing sliding scale of estate duty applicable where the donor of the shares dies within 4 to 7 years of making a gift.)

2 As already stated, your liability is limited in the event of failure of the business.

3 As a general rule, it is easier to obtain additional finance for a limited company than by a sole trader or partnership.

4 Continuity in the running of a limited company is unaffected by the death of a director or shareholder.

Disadvantages

1 The main disadvantage is that you must send a copy of the audited financial accounts to the Registrar of Companies, which means that any member of the public, by paying a small fee, can inspect them in addition to the documents required to be lodged before the company is incorporated. Against this, of course, the large income earners in British industry must now also disclose their annual salaries, and therefore it is very doubtful whether anyone will get excited over your comparatively small profits and salary.

2 A limited company must maintain a statutory register, which is also available to the public for their inspection. The statutory register must show:

a The shareholders of and their shareholdings in the company.
b The names and addresses of the directors and their shareholdings in the company.
c Brief details of any mortgage or charge entered into by the company in exchange for a secured loan.
d Details of the authorized and issued share capital.
e Details of any other directorships of the directors of the company.
f The name and address of the secretary.
A copy of the statutory register (known as the annual return) must be completed and submitted to the Registrar of Companies once a year, which is available to the members of the public for their inspection.

3 The accounts of a limited company must be audited. This means your accountant will not only have to prepare them but certify they are correct. In the case of a sole trader, the accounts only need be prepared from the books, receipts and other vouchers of the business.

2

4 A limited company must have a minimum of two shareholders. However, if you wish to own the company completely, then you can achieve this, at the same time complying with the law by the following method. Assume the company has an issued share capital of 1,000 ordinary shares of £1 each, fully paid. You retain 999 shares in your own name and issue 1 share to (say) your wife. You then obtain the signature of your wife to a blank Deed of Transfer for your completion at a later date if you so wish, at the same time asking her to sign a Declaration of Trust. This declaration will state that your wife is holding the share as your nominee and will act and vote in accordance with your wishes. The company will then be effectively, wholly owned by yourself.

It is always possible for you to change your method of trading from a sole trader or partnership to a limited company, or vice versa. It is recommended, however, that you only make such a move in consultation with your accountant as he will protect your interests as far as the Inland Revenue is concerned, as taxation problems can arise on a change of this nature.

CHAPTER 2

Setting Your Target

An excellent rule to apply in any situation involving an important decision is not to place yourself in a position of having to say yes or no to a proposal unless you have established well beforehand in your own mind an outline of what you hope to achieve. This is very true of buying a business. It does not mean to say that you should be too rigid in your aims, as the ideal or dream business rarely exists. On the other hand, your ideas should be definite enough to stop you being sidetracked into a trade or locality which is of no interest to you.

The main factors which you will consider will no doubt be the location of the business, the type of trade and, perhaps the greatest determining factor of all, your financial resources.

Location of Business

There is a wide selection to choose from as the location of a business can vary from densely populated town areas to remote villages, and again from High Streets to businesses located in secondary positions.

There are no hard and fast rules which can be applied to assessing one type of location against another except to say that a shop in a prime trading position ought to be the more profitable. To offset this, however, the cost of buying such a business may well be prohibitive if allowance is made for the cost of the lease of the property from which it trades, especially if the current rent is low compared with present day values. Alternatively, if a new lease of such a shop has recently been entered into, the rent could be in the region of £1,750 – £2,500 per annum or more. In these circumstances you could find your working capital severely depleted by paying the first rent instalment (usually quarterly in advance) before giving yourself the opportunity of building up an adequate and comprehensive range of goods to offer the shopping public.

With regard to other locations, in very general terms, a business in a town tends to be more profitable than one in a rural area, although there are many instances of businesses in the latter location doing as well as those located in urban areas.

If income is not your prime consideration, then no doubt you will have set your mind on a business in the country or a seaside resort, in which event the standard of the living accommodation may play an important part in your final decision. In these circumstances brace yourself to be patient, as quality businesses of this nature are in great demand and do not come onto the market very frequently.

Type of Trade

The golden rule to apply here is never to involve yourself in a business where it is possible to get out of your depth. Needless to say you should not contemplate a trade involving specialized knowledge or training which you do not possess, as it is true to say more money has been lost by people buying a business in a trade which they do not fully understand than for any other single reason. If you have set your mind on a particular trade but the buying of the business is not urgent, then time is on your side and you can make full use of it by either yourself or your wife finding full time or part time employment for a limited period in a shop of the same trade. You will then gain useful experience at someone else's expense, provided you do not fool yourself into believing that you will learn all there is to know about the trade.

Just as there is no family as the statistical average British family, it is equally true to say there is probably no such thing as the average shop. Over the years, however, the author has accumulated much information on a wide range of businesses, some of which is tabulated below as it may prove to be a useful guide when you find yourself in the situation of actually looking at accounts of a business in which you are interested.

Bear in mind when reading the table that it is based on a small sample and does not include shops situated in all types of locations and areas of the country, and must therefore be regarded only as an indication; and, secondly, do not confuse the meaning of gross profit with net profit, a subject which is dealt with in greater detail later.

	Average annual turnover	Average gross profit	Annual gross profit
	£	(Percentage)	£
Bakers	12,000	30	3,600
Butchers	16,000	20	3,200
Chemists	15,000	30	4,500
Coin operated launderettes	4,500	60	2,700
Cycles and accessories	7,000	25	1,750
Delicatessen	10,000	33	3,300
Drapers	9,000	25	2,250
Dry cleanery	6,000	45	2,700
Electrical goods	15,000	30	4,500
Fancy goods	8,500	35	3,000
Fishmongers	10,000	25	2,500
Greengrocers	8,000	20	1,600
Grocers	11,000	15	1,650
Ironmongers	10,000	25	2,500
Jewellers	9,000	30	2,700
Men's outfitters	15,000	30	4,500
Newsagents (including tobacco and confectionery)	12,000	15	1,800
Off licences	14,000	20	2,800
Shoe shops	9,000	25	2,250
Sports goods	9,000	30	2,700
Stationers	12,000	30	3,600
Women's clothing	9,000	30	2,700

You now realize that turnover of a business, although important, is meaningless in itself, as similarly is the percentage rate of gross profit. What is important is knowing both these figures to arrive at the gross profit of a business in terms of Sterling. On the basis of the above information, and as an example, if you saw an off licence for sale you may be very impressed on reading that its turnover is £270 per week. In fact the gross profit is only £100 per annum more than the average sports shop with a turnover of £170 per week, due to the latter achieving a higher margin of gross profit.

Finance

It is essential to calculate your potential financial resources so that you will have some idea of the maximum price range of business you can aim for and thus alleviate the necessity of wasting time and expense in travelling to look at businesses which are beyond your means. You will experience enough frustration without adding to the difficulties by looking at businesses which you cannot afford. First, you must assess how much cash you can raise from your own resources. If you own a house and propose to live in the accommodation attached to a business, you will be able to add the proceeds of sale, after deducting any outstanding building society mortgage, to your other savings to ascertain the total amount of capital you have available.

At this stage, you must consider whether to look for a business at a price in keeping with your own capital or, alternatively, to aim higher with the support of additional finance in the form of a loan. If the latter is the case, the first person to see is your bank manager. Irrespective of what many advertisements suggest, the cheapest money to borrow is undoubtedly an overdraft facility with one of the big banks. Bank managers, however, prefer specific proposals submitted to them for consideration, so that they can assess for themselves by looking at the accounts of the business the adequacy or otherwise of the security offered, and, more important, the anticipated level of profits out of which you must incur normal living expenses and repay their loan by instalments on due dates. Not having found a business, you cannot be specific at this point, but you can discuss the position generally with your bank manager and endeavour to obtain his support for the amount you have in mind, subject to his final approval when you have a business which interests you and are therefore able to present figures and discuss the position in greater detail.

Although banks require security, you can be assured that their prime consideration when advancing money is the question of repayment. It is not appreciated nearly enough that when a bank manager rejects a request for an overdraft where adequate security can be offered, he probably feels he is doing so more in your interest than his own on the grounds that too great a strain will be placed on you financially. Banks do not like the publicity and inconvenience which is associated with enforcing a security to enable them to repay themselves out of the proceeds.

Whether a bank manager is in a position to advance money at the time you submit your application may depend on instructions he has received from Head Office, who in turn may be in the hands of the Bank of England, depending on the economic position of the country; therefore, never take a rejection from a bank manager personally, as he may have no option other than to refuse you. On the other hand, never let it deter you from approaching any other bank with whom you have a connection, as they may be temporarily in a more fortunate position to accommodate you.

An alternative bank to approach at a later date is the one used by the vendor of the business in which you are interested. In many respects his bank has an advantage over your own as it will be in a better position to judge the potential and capabilities of the business to meet repayments on any loan granted to you. Banks loathe losing good accounts, and if the business you have in mind is sound, then they will do all they can to help you.

A bank usually requires repayment over a period of 5 years for a loan for the purchase of the trading assets, and repayment over 10–15 years on an advance to buy the freehold of the business, if available.

Assuming that you are unable to obtain assistance from one of the major banks, then there are other sources available. A remote possibility is that your solicitor may have a client who has money to invest and agrees to introduce you to him. Failing this, the usual source, after the commercial banks, will be one of the merchant banks who specialize in this type of loan. A mortgage broker will introduce you to one for a fee, or better still, if you were introduced to the business by a business transfer agent, he will have connections with and be able to introduce one to you. With regard to freeholds, if applicable, merchant banks advance money with a usual period of repayment of 10–12 years. Unfortunately, the majority of building societies will not help you, as their main function is to finance on mortgage the purchase of private dwelling houses. Occasionally you may be lucky with one of the smaller building societies if you already have a deposit account with them, and at the time of applying they have surplus cash available.

With regard to a loan to implement your capital to purchase a business other than the freehold, the usual maximum advance by a merchant banker is 50 per cent of the purchase price, excluding current assets (debtors and stock, etc.) repayable over a period of 3 to 5 years.

It may be suggested to you that a loan from the merchant banker to whom you are introduced is cheaper than one obtainable from the commercial banks, as the rate of interest may only be 5 per cent per annum after tax. A first impression is that it looks an attractive rate, but in reality the true interest rate is nearer 18 per cent per annum.

After tax, 5 per cent is approximately 9 per cent gross, which should be doubled as in the case of the rate of interest under a hire purchase agreement. The reason for this is that under a hire purchase agreement the gross rate of interest is calculated by taking the rate of interest on the original sum borrowed and multiplying it by the number of years over which the loan will be repaid. You are not borrowing the original sum for the whole of the period because each month you are reducing the loan, so the average loan is one half of the original sum. Therefore, 9 per cent on the original loan becomes 18 per cent per annum on one half of this figure.

To explain this by an example, take the following:

Loan repayable by equal monthly instalments over 4 years Interest
at 5% per annum net = 9% per annum gross (approx.)

Loan	£1,000
Interest £1,000 @ 9% = £90 per annum × 4 years	360
Total repayment	£1,360

The average interest is £90 per annum, the average borrowing over the 4 years is £500, therefore

$$\frac{900}{500} \times \frac{100}{1} = 18 \text{ per cent interest per annum.}$$

Bear in mind when budgeting for the repayment of a loan that the monthly instalments are payable out of income which is subject to taxation. As an indication, if the profit of the business is £30 per week (excluding a salary paid to your wife of £6 per week which will legitimately be tax free), a man and wife with no children will have to pay approximately £6 per week income tax leaving £24 a week out of the husband's salary or £30 per week including the wage of the wife to live on and repay the loan. In the above example, a loan of £1,000 at 5 per cent net repayable over 4 years will involve you in repayments of £340 per annum (£1,360 ÷ 4), or approximately £28 per month, including interest. This will be partially offset in due course by tax relief of £30 (approximately) per annum on the interest paid of £90 per annum over the 4 year period.

Another source of obtaining finance is to negotiate a loan from the vendor of the business, which, if agreed, can be simply arranged. When you have negotiated a price for the business, you will then offer so much cash payable on completion and the balance repayable to the vendor over an agreed period of time. You may have to pledge the business to the vendor as security for the sum he has loaned to you.

You should now be in a position to have an idea of the amount of finance you have available to cover the commitments involved in buying a business out of which you must pay for certain expenses and possibly set aside some cash for working capital.

A buyer is not responsible for paying the fee of the business transfer agent selling the business, as this is the vendor's responsibility. The purchaser will, however, have to pay for the services of his accountant, solicitor and surveyor, and possibly part of the cost involved in valuing the stock of the business as at the date of takeover, which may be undertaken by a specialist firm of surveyors or alternatively another firm of business brokers unconnected with the two parties. It is not possible to estimate how much your professional advisors will charge which must depend on the amount of time they spend on your affairs. With regard to the valuation of stock, the fee is usually $2\frac{1}{2}$ per cent of its value, and the common arrangement is for the buyer and vendor each to pay half.

You must also provide for stamp duty, which is payable to the Government Stamping Office at the time the signed agreement is submitted to them by either your own or the vendor's solicitor. The amount of duty will depend on the price you paid for the freehold property/lease (whichever is applicable) and goodwill. The agreement must be lodged for stamping, otherwise the provisions therein will not be enforceable at law in the event of a subsequent dispute arising between the parties.

The rate of duty payable is:

Up to £5,500	Nil
From £5,501 to £7,000	$\frac{1}{2}$%
From £7,001 and above	1%

You do not pay stamp duty on that part of the consideration which relates to the furniture, fittings, equipment, etc. and stock-in-trade.

At some stage you will be asked to substantiate your interest in the business by paying a deposit, the usual demand in this connection being 10 per cent of the asking price. This is a reasonable request as a vendor will not wish to indefinitely answer your questions and show you his books and other private papers unless he is satisfied that you are seriously considering the purchase of his business. The asking for a deposit does tend to eliminate those who are only half-hearted and thus saves his own time. Please note, however, the deposit should not be given to the vendor, but paid to an independent third person, who in turn will pass it onto the vendor in the event of completion, or return it to you if you fail to finalize the purchase. The usual practice is to pay the deposit to either the business broker who introduced you to the business, the bank of the vendor, your solicitor, or the solicitor of the vendor. When paying the deposit ensure that it is given subject to contract, and it should be acknowledged as such by the recipient. There are instances of a prospective purchaser paying a deposit without specifically stating that it is given subject to contract, and being obliged at a later date to complete the transaction even though he had no wish to do so. The alternative in these circumstances to completion would have been for the purchaser to have lost his deposit. The importance of leaving your solicitor to deal with all aspects involving the payment of a deposit cannot be overemphasized.

With regard to working capital, it is important to consider the retention of moneys to use as necessary in the business once you have acquired it. Many pressing demands can be made on your finances, one example being the possibility of a new shop front. You have noticed from past experience how clean smart shops seem to attract more custom than those which are dirty, drab and have untidy window displays. In addition, there are trades where profits can be substantially increased by taking advantage of all the cash discounts available by paying accounts on time. A shop in the shoe trade is an example.

You should now have a good idea of how much you can afford to pay for a business. It is suggested, however, you aim for a business with an asking price in excess of that which you can afford. As in the case of buying a house, the asking prices of businesses are fixed in the knowledge that they may be reduced during negotiations. In some instances where the business has been on the market for a long time and the vendor wishes to dispose of his business as quickly as possible, substantial reductions may be obtained by clever and persistent bargaining.

CHAPTER 3

Finding a Business

Just as some house owners try to sell their houses privately to save paying fees to estate agents, so do some vendors of businesses endeavour to dispose of them by inserting their own advertisements. Unfortunately, advertisements of this nature tend to be abbreviated as the vendor usually wishes to advertise as cheaply as possible and does not give much information on which to assess the business. All you will probably read is the location, the type of business and the weekly turnover; therefore if the information appears to be of interest to you, you can reply asking for further particulars. This method is not usually satisfactory from the buyer's point of view.

If you have set your mind on a type of business in a particular locality then you may consider the insertion of your own advertisement in the local papers servicing the area concerned. Once inserted, you can do no more than wait for replies, if any, and take them up from there.

The usual and most satisfactory method is to approach brokers who specialize in the field of selling businesses. There are numerous business transfer agents in existence and they frequently advertise their services in the national press and weekly advertising journals. Before approaching them, however, bear in mind that business transfer agents obtain their commission from the vendor and must have the interests of their clients more at heart than those of the purchaser. There does not appear to be a fixed scale of charges which business transfer agents apply, but a common one is 5 per cent of the selling price (excluding current assets) subject to a minimum of £250. Although business brokers will be willing to answer your questions, they may not be too informative to the detriment of the business you are enquiring after, otherwise they may continuously be talking themselves out of commissions and eventually out of business.

Once you have made up your mind to use the services of a business transfer agent, it is suggested you contact as many as possible, including those who have connections in the areas you have selected, at the same time giving them explicit details of your requirements, i.e. price range, standard of accommodation, type of trade, location, etc. The reason for this is, as explained earlier, under normal circumstances you may lose money and time in wasted journeys. Therefore, the more detailed your information the less your chance of looking at propositions which are of no interest.

Most agents appear to work on the basis of sending brief notes of all businesses they have available, at the same time offering to supply detailed information of those which particularly interest you. You will no doubt be inundated with circulars from which it will be necessary to make a short list by reading the literature and eliminating from it the businesses with no appeal and informing the broker of those which have. On receipt of the further information, go through the same process again until you are left with a few which appear to meet your requirements.

A point worth noting; in all probability on each page received from the broker will be a note to the effect that, although he believes the information to be true, the details shown will not form part of the final contract and he will not hold himself liable for any loss arising from erroneous information contained therein. You must prepare yourself for the fact, therefore, that sometimes the description of the business advertised may bear little resemblance to the one you actually see.

It is recommended that you only investigate one business at a time. If your first choice is the business you want, so well and good; if not, then go on to the second choice, and so on. This will avoid the necessity of involving yourself in more than one business at a time when it is very easy to lose track of events and cause yourself unnecessary complications and confusion.

If you have never had the experience of negotiating the purchase of a business, before seeing the vendor of your first choice you may like to consider the idea of selecting one or two local businesses which do not appeal to you and visiting them as a trial run. Ask the questions you think you ought to ask, pay attention to the answers, and generally get the feeling and atmosphere of negotiating without getting yourself too involved. After your visit think back over the events and consider how you could have improved on the method of your approach.

Finally, ascertain from the broker how long the business has been available for sale, because if it has been on the market for a considerable period of time it may suggest there is something wrong with it or, alternatively, it is overpriced. Unfortunately, some vendors are aware of this one and tend to pass the sale from broker to broker after short periods of time have elapsed to give the impression the business has only recently come onto the market.

CHAPTER 4

Your Method of Approach

At this point in the hypothetical chain of events of buying a business you will have selected the first business which interests you and may even have made an appointment with the vendor to see him.

It would do you no great harm to remind yourself now that you may be at the doorway of the most uneven contest you have ever entered into, and situations such as this sometimes evolve themselves into a battle of wits.

You already know the best features of the business without even seeing it, because they will have been referred to in the particulars supplied by the broker or advertisement. You will probably know the weekly turnover (always a nice round sum), whether the shop is freehold or leasehold, the weekly rent and unexpired period of lease, if applicable, and the margin of gross profit. You may also be told that the net profits are excellent (very seldom is the actual figure mentioned), and given an indication of the type of location in which the business is situated. You may even have been advised why the vendor wishes to sell the business, the usual reasons given being either the vendor wishes to emigrate or retire, has other more profitable business commitments or due to ill health, to name a few in a field which is unparalleled in its scope for ingenuity.

Trying to assess the value of a business by endeavouring to guess the real reason for sale is precarious under the most favourable of circumstances as the vendor may well have made his decision to sell some months or even years before and will have had an opportunity to steer his business into the lines which will support his reason for sale, assuming the reason given is not the real one. The vendor also has the advantage over you as he has worked the business for a period of time and knows the local conditions and gossip, the weaknesses of the shop in that given locality, and the trends. You could not go wrong by completely eliminating from your assessment of the business the reason given for sale.

The real reason for selling may indeed be due to emigration, retirement, etc., but there are many other reasons, as for example:

1 The vendor is aware of a new competitor opening nearby in the near future, possibly a multiple organization.
2 The premises may be required by the local authority for road widening purposes or other development at some future date.
3 The lease is due for renewal in the near future and the vendor has been told by the landlord of the rent required to renew the lease, which will be too high to continue to make a reasonable living. Alternatively, a new lease has recently been entered into at an uneconomical rent for that type of trade.
4 He 'bought a pup' and is trying to pass it on.
5 Declining trade.
6 Under the vendor's full repairing lease the landlord is insisting on certain expensive repairs and redecorations to be made in accordance with the terms of the lease.
7 He has, over a period of time, purchased stock unwisely which he now cannot easily liquidate, and does not have the financial resources to buy new stock so as to offer a good selection to his customers.
8 He may feel he would do better financially and have far less responsibility by selling up and taking salaried employment.

It is necessary that you find out any serious true reason for selling because and, as an example, if the reason is any one of those shown above it could have a strong bearing on your decision to buy and will certainly affect the price which you would be prepared to pay. Never be frightened of the vendor threatening to break off negotiations by your enquiries and probing, because he will realize that if you find any serious deficiency easily, so could anyone else who is introduced to him.

How do you find out? Most detrimental information about any business can be ascertained with reasonable ease. Of the possible reasons given (and there are many more) some of the points may be verified as undermentioned. The reasons against (3), (5) and (7) are not referred to as they are dealt with in greater detail later.

1 NEW COMPETITOR: Look at all the shops in the vicinity of the vendor and note those which are to let or which have been let. Telephone the agent shown on the board who is handling the disposal of the shop and endeavour to ascertain the trade of the

new lessee. Also talk to other local shopkeepers/assistants and find out the local gossip. Another possibility is to telephone the planning department of the local authority to see if a 'change of user' for the shop premises has been applied for.

2 ROAD WIDENING OR REDEVELOPMENT: This can be easily verified by contacting the local authority asking for development plans of the area. Most local authorities would answer you over the telephone. In some areas, however, there may be two authorities involved if there are road widening proposals. For example, the Greater London Council is usually responsible for the Ministry roads in Greater London Boroughs. If you do obtain an answer by telephone, you need not insist on written confirmation as your own solicitor will automatically do this for you if negotiations ever reach such an advanced stage.

3 BAD BUY: Make enquiries with other local shopkeepers as to when the business was last up for sale, or alternatively how long the vendor has had the business.

4 REPAIRS: There is not much you can do at this stage except to use your own judgement when looking over the property and asking the vendor outright whether there are any major repairs necessary at the same time drawing his attention to any obvious points requiring action. You can stress to the vendor that your solicitor will be asking the landlord at a later stage for a list of dilapidations and, in any event, you will have your own surveyor inspecting the property if the negotiations ever get so advanced.

The traditional advice of jumping on a bicycle and riding round the vicinity of the shop to see the standard of the area and estimating the spending capacity of your potential customers still applies, except that in these days it is supposed you will do so by car.

CHAPTER 5

Trading and Profit and Loss Account and Balance Sheet: a Sole Trader

The factor which will possibly influence you most of all when deciding whether or not to purchase a particular business will be the trading results as reflected by its annual financial accounts.

For reasons explained later it is advisable in the case of an old-established business for the prospective purchaser to inspect the most recent accounts and those of at least the preceding 5 years or, in the case of a business established within this period, to have sight of the accounts for the whole of the period since formation.

If the vendor implies that accounts have not been prepared, as occasionally happens, then it is suggested you immediately withdraw your interest for the reason that accounts must be submitted to the Inland Revenue for income tax (sole traders and partnerships) or corporation tax (limited companies) purposes to enable the Inspector of Taxes to assess the correct tax liability for any given period. If accounts are not prepared, the Inland Revenue estimate the tax payable by the taxpayer based on information supplied in earlier years and, not unnaturally, play for safety by demanding an excessive figure, leaving the taxpayer a choice of either paying the amount demanded or appealing to the Special Commissioners to have the assessment reduced with the aid of whatever other evidence he can produce. This method is so obviously to the detriment of a taxpayer that it can be safely assumed that accounts have been prepared but the vendor does not wish them to be seen for reasons which one can only suppose are to the detriment of his business.

As so many people buy a business without having even the most elementary knowledge of bookkeeping and accounts it is necessary to devote some attention to the subject and accordingly specimens of a shop trading account, profit and loss account and balance sheet are shown. The accounts are not intended to represent any particular trade, although they are more in keeping with those of a retail

3

Trading Account for the

	£
To Opening stock	3,465
Purchases	15,084
	18,549
Less : Closing stock	3,626
Cost of goods sold	14,923
Gross profit (24·3%) C/D	4,803
	19,726

Profit and Loss Account for the

	£
To Wages	984
Rent	550
General and water rates	282
Insurances	39
Lighting and heating	175
Telephone	34
Packaging materials	187
Printing and stationery	21
Postages	7
Motor expenses	236
Repairs to premises	146
Advertising	55
Bank interest and charges	10
Accountancy charges	35
Sundry expenses	96
Depreciation :	
Fixtures and fittings	55
Motor car	208
	3,120
Net profit for year	1,683
	4,803

Balance Sheet as at

	£
Capital Account	
Opening balance	5,538
Add : Profit for year	1,683
	7,221
Less : Drawings during year	1,539
	5,682
Current Liabilities	
Sundry creditors and accrued expenses	1,694
Bank overdraft	537
	7,913

Year Ended 31st December 19. .

	£
By Sales	19,726
	19,726

Year Ended 31st December 19. .

	£
By Gross Profit B/D	4.803
	4,803

31st December 19. .

	£	£
Fixed Assets		
Goodwill at cost		2,750
Fixtures and fittings at cost	1,100	
Less : Depreciation to date	495	605
Motor car at cost	1,040	
Less : Depreciation to date	416	624
		3,979
Current Assets		
Stock as valued by the proprietor		3,626
Sundry debtors and prepayments		226
Cash in hand		82
		7,913

business as compared with a business offering a service, e.g. ladies' hairdresser.

Reference was made earlier to a prospective purchaser inspecting the accounts of a business for at least a period of 5 years immediately prior to purchase, or the accounts of such lesser period prior to purchase in the case of a newly established business. The necessity for so doing is that the vendor may have decided to sell his business 2 or even 3 years beforehand and has taken the opportunity since making his decision to improve his trading results suitably by gradually increasing his turnover and profits over the period, leading up to the best trading results of all in the financial year immediately prior to sale.

This is not to suggest that you must automatically suspect a business showing both increasing turnover and profits, as there are obvious advantages in buying a genuinely expanding business, but you must be aware that it is possible to show these trends where the true position is one of stagnation or even decreasing trade. Taking an extreme view, even a business which in true terms is stagnant because each year it sells the same quantity of goods will show higher turnover and profits on the grounds of inflation alone. Trends of trading may be discounted in cases where a business is doing badly through obvious mismanagement by the existing proprietor through loss of enthusiasm, etc., and which can easily be rectified by applying the most elementary of good business methods to transform the business into an expanding one.

The specimen accounts previously shown are now elaborated in detail, which at the same time it is hoped will help you to understand their function.

Trading Account

The purpose of the trading account is to record the difference (known as gross profit) between the cost of goods purchased and the price at which they are sold, ignoring every other factor of expense which is considered in the profit and loss account.

In the example, the gross profit percentage of 24·3 per cent is ascertained by dividing the sales (£19,726) into the gross profit (£4,803) × 100. If the accounts presented to you do not show this information, then it is suggested you calculate the gross profit percentage of each set of accounts to build up a comparison over the period of review. There is a tendency for the gross profit percentage to show a small decline in some trades since the introduction of the Retail Price Maintenance Act. This trend may be discounted, however, if the fall has been accompanied by increasing turnover, which in turn reflects itself in a higher gross profit being made.

If during the early part of the 5 year period of review of accounts the gross profit percentage was falling and then rose sharply year by year to the present time, this may be indicative of the fact that the trading position has been adjusted with a view to sale and is one of the reasons for justifying the importance of seeing at least 5 years' accounts, if only to see the trend of the gross profit margin. One of the usual ways of achieving this fluctuation in the gross profit percentage is to undervalue the stock in the early years and then gradually write it up year by year to its true value in the year immediately prior to offering the business for sale. By way of elaboration, if the opening stock as reflected in the specimen accounts had been undervalued by £500 at £2,965, the gross profit would be £5,303 for the year (not £4,803) and the gross profit percentage 26·9 per cent (not 24·3 per cent), which gives a rosier picture of the business, even allowing for the detrimental effect the stock adjustment would have had on the results of the previous year.

You may properly ask the purpose of employing accountants if this sort of thing cannot be eliminated. The answer can lie with one of two reasons. As the business is in the ownership of a sole trader, and is therefore not trading as a limited company, the accountant has no responsibility to audit or attempt to verify the stock. Secondly, even if the stock was audited, of all the figures used to compile accounts the accountant must rely most heavily on the honesty and accuracy of the vendor for this information. It is no duty of the accountant to physically count the various items which comprise the stock as this task can only practically be undertaken by the vendor, who will do so on the last day of the financial year. By the time the accountant prepares the accounts two or more months may have elapsed since the year end, and it is then not possible for him to take sample checks on accuracy because purchases and sales will have taken place during the intermediate period. All the accountant can do with the stock sheets is to make sure the quantities appear to be in order, price the items of stock with invoices, and possibly test the quantities with stock record cards, if any. If the vendor has understated his stock, therefore, it is unlikely that the accountant will be able to prove the point although he may have his private reservations. Accountants invariably note against the stock item on the balance sheets of sole traders and partnerships that it was valued by the proprietor(s).

Although gross profit is an important indication to a purchaser, do not place too much reliance on it because, as you can see from the specimen accounts, many expenses have to be charged against gross profit in the profit and loss account before arriving at the net profit (or proprietor's income) for the year. Also remember a point made in an earlier chapter with regard to gross profit percentages; a gross profit of 17 per cent on a turnover of £500 per week (£85) is better than a gross profit of 30 per cent on a turnover of £200 per week (£60), assuming the expenses appearing in the profit and loss accounts are equal.

There are some trades where a generally accepted overall gross profit percentage is applicable, as for example the retailing of electrical goods with a traditional margin or mark-up value of 33⅓ per cent. If you inspect accounts of a shop in such a trade, it is possible for the overall gross profit margin to be less than the accepted working margin. The reason for this apparent disparity is that it is not always possible to sell at the accepted margin as even the best of buyers at times overstock on certain lines through undue optimism. Hence, one reason for the periodical sale is to clear these items at cut prices, i.e. reduced gross profit margins, to realize cash in order to purchase the more popular and therefore faster moving lines. In addition, the British spending public is becoming aware of cash discounts and is tending to ask for them more frequently. Both these factors, plus losses through pilferage, breakage, etc., will reduce the accepted overall margin of gross profit.

Profit and Loss Account

The function of this account is to offset the gross profit by charging those expenses which are not directly concerned with purchasing goods for subsequent resale. The balance of this account is either the net profit or net loss for the year. Unfortunately, so far as concerns profit and loss accounts, it is not possible to compare one business with another even within the same trade as the items of expense and amounts must depend on how much the proprietor wishes to spend in his particular circumstances and the emphasis he places on the various avenues of expenditure. For example the tenants of two shops adjacent to one another may be paying different rents, one proprietor may lay more importance on advertising than the other, one may have electric heating while the other is content to wear mittens, and so on.

Of the items shown in the specimen profit and loss account no hard and fast rules can be made; however, the following notes may be of interest.

Wages
Included in this figures may, on the advice of any accountant worth his salt, be included an amount of at least £300 per annum being salary paid to the wife for her services for assisting in the business. Any adult person is legally permitted to earn this sum before paying tax; therefore, by awarding the wife £300 per annum no tax is payable; whereas, if the husband retained the £300 to increase his own income, and if he pays tax at the standard rate, he will have an unnecessary but additional tax burden of £100 per year. You need have no qualms about enquiring into this personal matter. The vendor will no doubt beat you to it by informing you that this is happening without having to ask, as it will effectively increase the annual net profit of the business by the amount paid. You can, if you wish, ask to see the relevant P.A.Y.E. deduction card and receipts to ensure that it is so, as the gross pay will be recorded if the amount is being paid to the wife.

As the business is not a limited company, beware of the vendor really trying to impress you by claiming that his own salary is included in the item of wages. The salary of the proprietor is the net profit and no amount paid to him can be shown in the wages account. What may happen is that he withdraws cash each week out of the business to pay current living expenses in anticipation of his net profit which will not be known until the financial year ends. These withdrawals are known as drawings and will be shown as such on the balance sheet per example as a deduction from capital account.

Rent
This item can cause serious miscalculation on the part of those inexperienced in dealing with shop rents. Assume the financial year ends on the 31st December, and on the 1st January following a new

lease is entered into, or an increasing rent revision clause is applied to bring the rent into line with the current market value of (say) £1,000 per annum. This will mean an increased cost to the business of £450 per annum over the rent as shown in the specimen profit and loss account. All other factors of trading being equal in the subsequent year, the profit will fall from £1,683 to £1,233. It will take a substantial increase in turnover at a gross profit of 24·3 per cen to offset the additional rental; to be precise, an increase of turnover of £1,800 or 9 per cent for the year is necessary. You must allow for this and similar unavoidable adjustments in the purchase price by reducing the valuation on goodwill, which will be calculated on the basis of adjusted net profit.

You should also bear this point in mind if the lease is to terminate or a rent revision clause is to apply in the near future. If the former is the case, and the landlord has not yet indicated the new rental, you should instruct your surveyor to assess what it may be, thus allowing you the opportunity of calculating the likely effect on the profit and loss account should you buy the business.

General and Water Rates

Most people are aware of the nature of these two items and that an occupier of property has no control over the amount levied by the local authority and Water Board. In the event of acquiring business premises with the intention of building an extension or undertaking other improvements, you will have to accept that the local authority will increase the rateable value of the property on the grounds that its amenities have been improved.

Insurances

The question of insurances is dealt with in greater detail in a later chapter, and no reference will be made here except to draw your attention to a tendency by proprietors to economize on insurance premiums. This attitude has been regretted by many a proprietor at a later stage when a claim has arisen. A sole trader's greatest asset is usually his business and he should accordingly always have regard to this by adequately safeguarding himself against all relevant insurable risks.

Motor Expenses

There is a tendency for all motor expenses of a proprietor, including those incurred for private use, to be charged to his business account and a purchaser may accordingly be under the impression that they are all allowable for income tax purposes. The vendor may encourage this view. It is probable, however, that in the proprietor's personal income tax computation the Inspector of Taxes may adjust the computation by adding back to the income on which tax is paid that element of motor car expense which related to private use.

Repairs to Premises

A prospective purchaser should particularly note in the accounts over the 5 year period the expenditure the vendor has incurred year by year on maintaining his premises. Repairs are always necessary to property to maintain it in good order; therefore, if little or no expenditure has been incurred during the 5 years, you should ensure your surveyor reports specifically on the condition of the property and gives an estimation of the cost of putting the premises into a good state of repair to accord with the terms of the lease. It has already been mentioned that one reason why the vendor may be selling is that he knows a great deal of expenditure is necessary to the premises on major items, such as repairs to roof, structural repairs, or replacement of timbers due to woodworm, wood fungi, etc.

Depreciation

Fixed tangible assets, such as fixtures and fittings and motor cars, are wasting assets, that is they only have a limited useful life at the end of which they must be replaced by new. Depreciation is, therefore, an annual charge or rental against profits for the use of the assets by the business to retain sufficient funds, so that when the assets are replaced cash is available to cover the cost of replacement.

Any standard accountancy textbook will explain several methods for providing for depreciation, but the two most commonly used are the 'reducing balance method' and the 'straight line method'. Both methods achieve the desired result, but they are different in their application and have a varying effect on the profits of a business.

Reducing Balance Method

The basic principle of this method is that in the year of purchase of any fixed asset an agreed percentage of the cost is deducted by way of depreciation, leaving a written-down value. At the end of the second year the same percentage rate for depreciation is again applied, this time to the written-down value of the previous year. This will continue year by year until the asset is scrapped, and results in the charge for depreciation each year in the profit and loss account being a reducing one. The theory underlying the reducing balance method is that, as the charge for depreciation reduces, so the asset becomes older, and accordingly the cost of maintaining it increases. Over a period of time the combined charge to the profit and loss account for depreciation and repairs should be consistent.

If during the 5 year period of accounts there have been no additional purchases of the same class of fixed asset, but the charge for depreciation year by year is a reducing figure, then you can safely assume that it is this method which is being applied. To calculate the annual rate of depreciation under the reducing balance method, the following formula should be used:

$$\frac{\text{Depreciation charged for the year}}{\text{Written down value of asset at beginning of year}} \times \frac{1}{100}$$

Referring to fixtures and fittings as shown in the balance sheet of this chapter, the rate of depreciation is:

	£
Written down value at end of year	605
Depreciation charged in profit and loss account	55
Written down value at beginning of year	660

$$\text{Therefore, } \frac{55}{660} \times \frac{100}{1} = 8\tfrac{1}{3}\% \text{ per annum}$$

Straight Line Method

The principle of this method is that a fixed percentage is applied for depreciation to the original cost each year; it follows, therefore, that the charge for depreciation will be consistent year by year, and if this is so in the accounts for the period of 5 years you will readily recognize that it is this method which is being used. The annual rate of depreciation being applied in writing-off the two fixed assets shown in the specimen accounts in this chapter are calculated as follows:

Fixtures and fittings

$$\frac{\text{Annual depreciation}}{\text{Cost of asset}} \times \frac{100}{1} = \frac{55}{1,100} \times \frac{100}{1} = 5\% \text{ per annum}$$

Motor car

$$\frac{208}{1,040} \times \frac{100}{1} = \underline{\underline{20\% \text{ per annum}}}$$

Net Profit

This will undoubtedly be from your point of view the most important and interesting feature of the profit and loss account, as you will use the net profit figure to calculate its adequacy to cover both living expenses and loan repayments. You may adjust the profit to allow for any obvious increase you will be able to achieve by improving the running of the business if you can see clearly that its potential has not been fully exploited, or alternatively, if you can visualize economies in running costs where the vendor is obviously over-spending. In your own interest do not be too ambitious in estimating the extent of any increase in profits, because they often take longer to achieve than was originally contemplated.

Also note the trend of profits over the period of 5 years; that is, whether the trend is upwards or vice versa, or whether the profit fluctuates year by year.

Balance Sheet

The purpose of the balance sheet is to show the financial position of the business or, to express it in another way, what the business owns and owes.

Referring to the fixed assets first as shown in the balance sheet, we find the following points.

Goodwill
Goodwill is perhaps the most difficult asset of all to explain, as it is not represented by anything which is tangible as in the case of fixtures and fittings or a motor car. Goodwill has been defined in law as 'The benefit arising from connection and reputation' or 'The probability that the old customers will resort to the old place'. It is implied in the two definitions that contributing factors in assessing its value

are the location and standard of the shop, the type of trade, the profits achieved, the quality of goods sold and the class of clientele.

Another way of expressing goodwill is the advantage a purchaser of an established business has over an individual who starts one by leasing a shop in a newly developed parade. There are obvious uncertainties in starting a new business, as the shop must be decorated and fitted out, usually at considerable cost; it must be established in the area by getting the business, its products and the personality of the proprietor widely known as quickly as possible to build up a reasonable level of turnover; stock must be purchased with full awareness of the true needs of the public in the locality, and so on. During this initial and testing period trading losses may be incurred, or at best only a small profit made, and the owner may find it difficult to live on and pay his business expenses without additional support from his banker.

Goodwill may also embrace the value of the lease attached to the business. This alone can be valuable under certain circumstances, as in the case of a lease with a rent of £250 per annum with 12 years unexpired when the current market rental value is £600. The value of the lease may be anything between £2,000 and £3,000, depending on the condition of the premises and the location of the shop.

The goodwill on the specimen balance sheet is shown as £2,750. This value need not necessarily apply to you as a buyer, as it was the price to the vendor at the time when he originally acquired the business and may have fluctuated in value since then. If he paid too much for the goodwill in the first place, or if he has allowed the trade to deteriorate over the years, then it must be his loss if the value has fallen. On the other hand, if the goodwill is now worth more, then it is to the vendor's benefit to compensate him for the hard work and energy he has put into the business to make it more successful.

Fixtures and Fittings

It is a relevant exercise from a buyer's point of view to calculate on an average life basis when the tangible fixed assets were originally purchased so that a realistic price can be offered for them. A calculation has already been shown in this chapter to ascertain the rate of depreciation being used to write off the two assets appearing in the specimen balance sheet and the results may now be partially used to calculate the average age of the fixtures and fittings thus:

Reducing Balance Method

		£
Written down value (per balance sheet)		605
Depreciation (per profit and loss account)		55
Written down value	Year 1	660

Depreciation $8\frac{1}{3}\% = \dfrac{1}{12}$

$\dfrac{1}{12 - 1} = \dfrac{1}{11}$ of £660   60

Written down value	Year 2	720

Depreciation $\dfrac{1}{11}$ of £720   65

Written down value	Year 3	785

Depreciation $\dfrac{1}{11}$ of £785   71

Written down value	Year 4	856

Depreciation $\dfrac{1}{11}$ of £856   77

Written down value	Year 5	933

Depreciation $\dfrac{1}{11}$ of £933   85

Written down value	Year 6	1,018

Depreciation $\dfrac{1}{11}$ of £1,018   92

Original cost £1,100	Year 7	£1,110

Straight Line Method

$$\frac{\text{Depreciation to date}}{\text{Annual depreciation}} = \frac{495}{55} = 9 \text{ years}$$

This suggests that the average life of the fixtures and fittings is 7 years if the reducing balance method applies or 9 years under the straight line method. Note the words 'average life' because part of the fixtures and fittings could be 15 years old while others are only 5 years. Also, some of the fixtures and fittings may have been second-hand when purchased by the vendor. The importance of the calculation will be fully realized if the vendor claims he only purchased the fixtures and fittings 4 years previously, as he may attempt to do and therefore expect a '4 year' price.

Motor Car
The same formulae apply here, making the motor car just under 2 years old by repeating the first calculation and exactly 2 years old by the second.

Current Assets
In the layout of current assets in a balance sheet, it is usual to find that, the nearer the item is to cash, the lower in order the asset goes. Referring to the specimen balance sheet, cash is the lowest item, sundry debtors and prepayments are next because once the account is paid it becomes cash with stock becoming either a debtor or cash when sold and, therefore, appearing as the third item from the bottom.

Current assets are by their nature items which arise from trading.

It is unusual to have a high figure for sundry debtors in a balance sheet of a retail shop which has predominantly a cash basis of trading.

A prepayment is an expense paid in advance of the liability arising. An example in relation to the accounts shown would be the payment of rates in October of (say) £130 for the 6 months ending on the following 31st March. The prepayment is £65 covering the period 1st January to the said 31st March, i.e. one half of £130.

Liabilities

Capital Account
The balance of the capital account (£5,682) represents the proprietor's money invested in the business. It could be wholly represented by cash paid in from the proprietor's private account, or wholly represented by accumulated profits retained in the business. In practice, it will probably be a combination of the two.

You will notice in the specimen balance sheet that the net profit for the year has been added to the opening balance of the capital account and deducted therefrom are the proprietor's drawings as mentioned earlier. From the income tax position it will make no difference whether the proprietor withdraws all his profits in cash for his own private purposes or leaves part of them in the business to finance future expansion; income tax will be paid on the total profits made for the year.

The capital account at the year end of £5,682 also represents the 'net worth' of the business; that is, if all the fixed and current assets were realized at the same value as shown in the balance sheet, and all liabilities totalling £2,231 (creditors £1,694 plus overdraft £537) were settled, it would leave exactly £5,682 in the business bank account available to the proprietor to transfer to his own private account.

Current Liabilities

Sundry Creditors and Accrued Expenses
Sundry creditors represent the liabilities which have been incurred to buy goods or services on a short term credit basis, usually to be paid for within 30 days from date of receipt of goods or invoice, and remaining unpaid on the 31st December. Accrued expenses are liabilities similar to rents or subscriptions payable on fixed dates in arrear in respect of the unpaid amount from the expiry of the previous payment to the financial year end.

Bank Overdraft
It is sometimes thought that a bank overdraft, the limit of which will have been previously determined between the vendor and his bank manager, is always available to a business. In practice, this may be so in the case of well managed businesses, but technically, a bank usually retains the right in the agreement to seek full repayment of an overdraft on demand.

CHAPTER 6

Trading and Profit and Loss Account and Balance Sheet: a Partnership

The legal distinction between a partnership and sole trader has already been drawn in Chapter 1, namely, whereas the sole trader is the proprietor, a partnership is a business undertaken by two or more people. This essential difference, therefore, must be reflected in the preparation and presentation of accounts of a partnership to conform with those sections of the Partnership Agreement relating to capital accounts, division of profits and drawings by partners.

The accounts presented in Chapter 5 will be used to show the specimen presentation of accounts of a partnership only to the extent of the variations which are necessary to explain the division of profits between the partners by incorporating the use of a profit and loss (appropriation) account and their respective capital and current accounts. The trading and profit and loss accounts and balance sheet (other than the top left hand corner) will be as already shown in Chapter 5 in all respects and you will be able to follow on from the net profit of £1,683 for the year.

A Partnership
Profit and Loss (Appropriation) Account

	£		£
To Division of profit		By Net profit for the	
Partner A	842	year brought down	1,683
Partner B	841		
	1,683		1,683

The profit and loss appropriation account shows the division of profits between partners A and B (to the nearest £1). If the Partnership Agreement provides for salaries payable to partners, they would be shown in this account; similarly interest allowed or charged on partners' capital and current accounts and drawings.

Balance Sheet as at 31st December 19..

	£	£
(TOP LEFT)		
Capital accounts		
Partner A	2,500	
Partner B	2,500	5,000
Current accounts		
A Opening balance	300	
Share of profit	842	
	1,142	
Less : Drawings	920	222
B Opening balance	238	
Share of profit	841	
	1,079	
Less : Drawings	619	460
		5,682

The top left hand corner of the balance sheet provides for the fixed capital of each partner, which may only be increased or reduced as the partners mutually agree in accordance with the terms of the Partnership Agreement, leaving the annual fluctuations arising from the crediting of the respective partners' share of profit and the debiting of drawings to the current accounts.

The total of the capital and current accounts of £5,682 is the net worth of the partnership, the definition of which has already been referred to in the previous chapter.

Perhaps the only other relevant factor which need be mentioned so far as concerns a partnership balance sheet is the valuation of goodwill if appearing in the accounts. It is advisable to note the value of this asset in each balance sheet during the period of review and ascertain whether it has varied at any time. It is possible to achieve an artificially inflated worth for goodwill on the admittance and resignation of partners which can be no more than bookkeeping exercises and unrelated to the true position or value. The value of goodwill of a business as valued by the partners is of no concern to a purchaser who is only concerned with its worth to him, personally.

CHAPTER 7

Trading and Profit and Loss Account and Balance Sheet: a Limited Company

It is no duty of this book to turn you into accountants and no doubt by now you are beginning to feel weary of the subject, but try to bear with this chapter if only to complete the process of being able to recognize accounts arising from the three main forms of trading. You may have to deal with a vendor who is trading as a limited company.

Under these circumstances, a purchaser has two alternatives. He can buy the trade and fixed assets (including lease and goodwill) of the limited company or buy the share capital. This distinction may seem a technicality, but in fact is important enough to tabulate the main advantages and disadvantages of each method.

Buying Trade and Fixed Assets

The purchaser is relieved of the legal responsibility of collecting debts and paying liabilities for his own account which arose before acquisition and thus eliminating the possibility of:

1 Suffering loss by non-recoupment of debts payable to the company through bad debts.
2 Having to pay expenses of which he was not aware at the time of purchase due to the vendor having suppressed invoices.

This will not preclude an arrangement commonly made between vendor and purchaser on buying only the trade and fixed assets of a limited company, and that is if the latter should receive money to which the vendor is entitled, then the purchaser accepts it and remits the cash to the vendor after deducting and retaining 5 per cent, or whatever other percentage is agreed, as a handling fee.

Buying Share Capital

The advantage here is that the purchaser will be able to continue using the trading name of the business as this will form part of the assets subject to the sale. Assume the business is called J. Smith & Co. Ltd.; if the purchaser buys only the trade, etc., then the vendor retains the right in the name, although the purchaser may, if he so wishes, incorporate a company and trade under the name of J. Smith (1969) & Co. Ltd., or some name similar thereto. If the purchaser buys the share capital, he may continue to trade as J. Smith & Co. Ltd.

The main disadvantage is the converse mentioned earlier; namely, if any debts due to the business subsequently become bad debts, the purchaser must stand the loss; likewise he will also have to pay for any unexpected bills incurred by the vendor and not known to the purchaser at time of takeover. To counteract this situation, the author has known of instances where the purchaser has withheld part of the purchase price from the vendor, with prior agreement, out of which he has met losses of this nature and remitted the balance to the vendor after an agreed period of time.

Reference will again be made to the specimen accounts in Chapter 5 as the distinction is only a question of layout arising from legal requirements. There is no need to reproduce the trading account which remains as shown.

Profit and Loss Account

With regard to the profit and loss account, you must be reminded that the proprietor of a limited company is one of its servants even though a director, and any salary he awards himself will be shown in this account as directors' remuneration, as will appear all salaries and wages of other employees except they will be shown under separate headings. If the wife is also a director of the company, then her wage should be deducted from the heading of wages in the specimen account and added to directors' remuneration.

All other items of expenses in the profit and loss account of the sole trader will appear in this account under directors' remuneration and in the same order.

A Limited

Profit and Loss Account for the

	£
To Directors' remuneration (hitherto drawings)	1,539
Other expenses (they will be tabulated in the same order as previously shown)	3,120
	4,659
Net profit for year (£1,683 − £1,539 Directors' remuneration) C/D	144
	4,803

Profit and Loss

	£
To Final dividend (proposed)	50
Corporation tax	75
Balance carried to balance sheet	2,557
	2,682

A Limited

Balance Sheet as at

	£	£
Authorized share capital		
5,000 ordinary shares, of £1 each	5,000	
Issued share capital		
3,000 ordinary shares of £1 each fully paid		3,000
Profit and loss account		2,557
		5,557
Corporation tax		75
Current liabilities		
Sundry creditors and accured expenses		1,694
Dividend—proposed		50
Bank overdraft		537
		7,913

Profit and Loss (Appropriation) Account

This account, as its name implies, deals with the distribution of and retention in the business of profits, once established. Liability for corporation tax on profits should be debited to this account, and similarly dividends declared on the ordinary issued share capital payable to shareholders.

Company
Year Ended 31st December 19..

	£
By Gross profit B/D	4,803
	4,803

(Appropriation) Account

	£
By Balance brought forward from 1st January 19..	2,538
Net profit for year B/D	144
	2,682

Company
31st December 19..

	£	£
Fixed assets		
Goodwill at cost		2,750
Fixtures and fittings at cost	1,100	
Less : Depreciation	495	605
Motor Car at cost	1,040	
Less : Depreciation	416	624
		3,979
Current assets		
Stock at lower of cost or market value		3,626
Sundry debtors and prepayments		226
Cash in hand		82
		7,913

Balance Sheet

Authorized Share Capital
The authorized share capital is the maximum permitted amount of
capital which can be issued by directors of a company to raise cash
for purposes of expansion until such time as the authorized capital
is increased in the manner to comply with the Memorandum and

Articles of Association of the company. It is usually provided in the Articles for the passing of a special resolution by shareholders at a meeting specially convened for this purpose.

Issued Share Capital

The issued share capital is the amount of capital which has been raised by a company. The issued share capital can be equal to or less than the authorized capital, but under no circumstances can it exceed the authorized share capital. The nominal amount of capital subscribed for by shareholders represents the maximum loss which they can individually suffer in the event of failure of the company.

Although the information appearing in these accounts is basically the same as shown in the previous two examples, the net worth of the limited company is only £5,557 as compared with £5,682. The difference in net worth is accounted for by the limited company being liable, in its own right, for the payment of corporation tax (£75) and the proposed dividend of £50, factors which do not affect the businesses of either a sole trader or partnership. Taxation is the personal liability of a sole trader or partner, and the declaration of dividends does not apply to non-limited company forms of trading.

CHAPTER 8

Leases

Following the subject of accounts, the second most important feature of a business must be the terms and conditions applying to the lease of the premises which the business occupies, as the worth of the business must largely depend on them. This point cannot be over-emphasized. If you take an extreme view, you will not wish to buy a business and discover at a later date that the lease is for all intents and purposes a worthless piece of paper, rendering the whole of your capital investment to nothing.

The purpose of this chapter is to give you an elementary under-standing of the subject, at the same time stressing the need of the services of a solicitor to fully advise you and to protect your in-terests before committing yourself to purchase.

It will be unusual if a vendor permits you to take away his lease for you to read at your leisure as it is a valuable document, but he may have a copy for this purpose or, alternatively, he can obtain one for you.

A standard type of shop lease provides for the following:

1 The name and address of the landlord.

2 The name and address of the tenant.

3 The date on which the lease was signed.

4 The date of commencement and duration of the lease.

5 The annual rent payable. Have particular regard to this clause if it contains provisions for an adjustment of rent at fixed intervals during the lease, which may result in a higher rent being demanded from the tenant. A common rent revision clause in a 21 year lease provides for an increased rent on the expiration of 7 and 14 years. Your attention has already been drawn to the effect on profits by a substantial increase in rent.

This clause will also state whether the rent is exclusive or inclusive of other outgoings. In practical terms, you will normally find that the rent is exclusive, leaving the tenant to pay general and water rates, together with a wide provision for the tenant to pay any other Government taxes if and when they are legislated for by Act of Parliament.

6 The dates on which rent is payable, for example each quarter day in advance.

There may then follow a series of undertakings on the part of the tenant which he must conform to, the most important being:

1 To pay the rent on due dates.

2 To pay all rates and other outgoings when demanded.

3 If a full repairing lease, provision will be made for the tenant to maintain the premises in a good state of repair both internally and externally, the usual obligation being for the outside to be painted in a workmanlike manner every 3 years and the interior every 7 years.

4 To comply with all local and national Government laws affecting shop properties, including an obligation on the part of the tenant to apply to the appropriate planning authority if major alterations to the property are contemplated, after first obtaining permission from the freeholder.

5 To permit the landlord or his agent to inspect the premises during reasonable hours to note the condition of the property and to effect repairs at the tenant's expense if the tenant fails to carry out his repair obligations in a satisfactory manner.

6 If the tenant must insure the property and the risks to be covered. (Occasionally provision is made for the landlord to be responsible for fire insurance on the building at the expense of the tenant.)

7 Provision as to the tenant's right to sublet. This is also an important clause, as in all probability the vendor will be subletting or assigning the property to the purchaser. A normal clause in this respect is for

the tenant not to sublet the property without first obtaining the landlord's permission, which cannot unreasonably be withheld. The purpose of this is to allow the landlord the opportunity to refuse permission if he considers, with justification, that his new tenant will be an undesirable person or one who will not be able to pay the agreed rent.

8 Provision as to the type of trades which can be undertaken on the premises. From the point of view of the tenant, the wider this right the better, as a restrictive covenant can cause complications at a later stage in the event of the tenant desiring to sell his interest in the lease, due to the nature of the area changing to such a degree that there is no longer a demand for the particular trade he is engaged in.

9 The right of the landlord to advertise the premises to let during the duration of the lease by attaching a board to the exterior of the premises in the event of the tenant indicating that he will not renew.

Covenants on behalf of the landlord usually then follow, the important one being that, provided the tenant properly fulfils his obligations, he will be permitted to 'peaceably and quietly hold and enjoy the premises'.

A note which may prove to be of interest to a purchaser is whether the name of the vendor appears on the lease as the tenant. If not, you will know that the business has changed hands at least once and that an assignment of the lease must be in existence.

Reference must now be made to the position of a tenant on the termination of a shop lease. Fortunes have been made by the legal profession on this subject, and no doubt will continue to be made arising from the volumes of legal books and many Acts of Parliament dealing with the relationship existing between a shop tenant and his landlord. Perhaps an oversimplified summary of the position would be that a tenant of a shop has a measure of legal protection on the termination of his lease, although his rights in this respect are not so extensive as those of a tenant of a residential dwelling. Generally, but subject to exceptions referred to later, a business tenant must be offered a new lease on similar terms and conditions as prevailing under the old lease, subject only to a current market rent being substituted for the old rent, which may be completely unrealistic in accordance with today's values, and the duration of the lease being for a reasonable period if the original lease was of long duration. A reasonable period for a lease is now considered to be 21 years.

A landlord's view of a current market rent very seldom matches that of a tenant; therefore, if the landlord asks for a rent which in the opinion of the tenant is too high, the tenant will be perfectly within his rights to say so and negotiate accordingly. In the event of the tenant and landlord failing to arrive at an amicable arrangement, both tenant and landlord have the right to apply to a third party to act as arbitrator to resolve the matter for them.

The exceptions referred to under which a landlord can obtain possession of his property and, therefore, not grant a new lease are:

1 If the tenant has committed a serious breach of the repair covenant. Emphasis is placed on the word 'serious', because the landlord will not be able to substantiate his claim by producing a list of minor repairs requiring attention. For example, it would be doubtful if a landlord could gain possession by proving that the exterior had not been painted during a particular year.

2 Persistent and serious delays by the tenant in paying his rent.

3 Any other serious breach of the lease by the tenant. Again, the landlord would not gain possession by presenting details of minor infringements. An example of a serious breach would be if the landlord could show the tenant to be using or permitting the use of the premises for immoral purposes.

4 If the landlord offers and is able to provide similar alternative shop accommodation in the area on equal terms as at present prevailing, subject only to rent and duration of lease as already referred to.

5 If the tenant is only occupying part of the premises, the remainder being vacant, the landlord may be able to gain possession to enable him to offer the shop as a whole.

6 If the landlord wishes to, and subsequently does, demolish the premises for redevelopment purposes.

7 If the landlord wishes to and can subsequently show that he occupied the premises for his own use.

CHAPTER 9

Taxation

How should you be influenced if the vendor, in endeavouring to justify his price, suggests with a wink and a grin that the accounts represent only part of the story, because in addition to the turnover as shown in the accounts cash is retained on which income tax is not paid?

It is not the author's intention to pass moral judgement on actions of this nature, or to encourage them. Obviously tax avoidance is contrary to law, and will no doubt always remain so, accompanied by severe financial penalties and/or lengthy terms of imprisonment to those experiencing the misery of back-duty procedure where the courts find in favour of the Inland Revenue.

On the other hand, no book on the subject of buying a business can omit to mention the problem, as tax avoidance is practised, and from the point of view of a purchaser suggestions of tax avoidance will undoubtedly be mentioned by the vendor.

Although tax avoidance is no doubt practised by a large percentage of retailers with a cash trade, the amount involved may be overestimated. Fortunately for those who participate in this human failing, they are reasonably safe from a questionnaire from the Board of Trade on the subject, as even the Statistical Office of that august body would recognize the results may not be representative of the true position, even if seasonally adjusted.

If we may refer once again to the question of gross profit percentages, the Inland Revenue maintain a table of gross profit margins usually associated with each trade. If accounts are presented to them showing an outrageously low gross profit margin, the trader concerned, or his accountant, will be subjected to a considerable volume of correspondence before the Inland Revenue will accept the accounts for the purpose of computing the tax liability.

If you refer to the specimen trading accounts shown in Chapter 5, calculate for yourself the effect on the gross profit percentage if £1,200 was withheld from turnover and retained by the trader. The

Inland Revenue are very conscious of the fact that when inspecting accounts they are at a disadvantage, due to the volume of work they have to attend to and the limited time available, and they make full use of any information which begs further investigation.

If the vendor has avoided tax in the past, he may have decided 2 or 3 years before sale to be an honest citizen by banking all his takings to give an impression of expanding turnover and increasing profits to justify a higher asking price for his business. The vendor will realize he will pay more income tax, but will anticipate a higher price for his business to offset his spirit of generosity.

From a purchaser's point of view, there is nothing a vendor can do to satisfy you that he has been avoiding tax, and you should accordingly ignore this factor in your calculations. The vendor can show you a second set of books—but anybody can prepare them. He could show you a mattress full of £5 notes—but he could be the type of person who simply lacks trust in banks. You should make up your mind at the outset, therefore, that the vendor cannot have it both ways. If he wants to avoid tax, then the price must be fixed to exclude the benefit of the takings retained by him. If he wants a better price, he must show the true takings which in turn will reflect itself in the accounts shown to you. More poor businesses have been sold at an exorbitant price on the strength of non-existent tax avoidance than for any other single reason.

A true position may be that there is less tax avoidance in a poor business than in a good one. If the wife receives £300 per year, then there is no point in withholding cash from a business if it only makes £700 or less a year, as the tax payable on this sum will not be excessive, if any liability will arise at all after deduction of personal allowances, and it is certainly not worth risking severe penalties for.

Another feature of this sort of situation is when the vendor suggests that he lives on the premises rent free, rate free and charges all his personal light and heat, telephone and motor car expenses to the business. If you look at the specimen profit and loss account shown earlier, you may accept this as fact, as all the expenses are debited to the business account. This is not necessarily so. The Inland Revenue add back to the profit a proportion for private use of all expenses which are jointly business and private on which tax is paid. The view of the author is, however, that the Inland Revenue are reasonable on this question, to the extent at times of being generous in the amount of expenses they accept for private use.

How this is achieved may be seen from the following specimen tax computation, which ignores the salary to the wife of £6 per week which is tax free.

A Sole Trader

INCOME TAX COMPUTATION

(This computation is based on the specimen accounts shown in Chapter 5)

	£	£
Profit as per accounts		1,683
Add		
Proportion of expenses for private use, i.e. heat, light, rent, etc.	150	
Private use of motor car	100	
Depreciation of fixtures and fittings	55	
Depreciation of motor car	208	513
		2,196
Less		
Annual allowance : fixtures and fittings	40	
Annual allowance : motor car	170	210
		1,986
Less		
Interest on private loan		90
		1,896
Less		
Earned income allowance	422	
Married (personal) allowance	340	762
		1,134

Income tax will be paid on £1,134 for the year, not all of which will be payable at the standard rate of income tax as reduced rates are effective on part of the taxable income.

The figures shown in the computation will not necessarily apply, as the purpose of the computation is to show the principle. The proprietor may well have other expenses which are allowable for tax purposes.

The living and car expenses will be charged by the Inland Revenue in accordance with how much the proprietor claims it has cost him for personal use, but the purchaser of the business will have to remember that the Inland Revenue will have knowledge of how much was claimed by the previous owner.

By way of explanation, depreciation for fixtures and fittings, and for the motor car, are added back as businesses in general apply differing rates and methods for calculating depreciation. In lieu of depreciation, the Inland Revenue grant annual capital allowances, which are standard rates for similar classes of assets to reduce all businesses to a common basis for tax purposes.

If a vendor permits you to see his personal income tax computation, look for the amount the Inland Revenue added back for his private living expenses.

Accounts: Current Period

However thoroughly the financial history of a business is investigated, it must be appreciated there will be a period of trading unsupported by financial accounts, covering the interval between the most recent financial year end for which accounts have been prepared and the date of the prospective purchaser's introduction to the business.

If the approach is 3 months after a financial year end, and the vendor employs a conscientious but not overburdened accountant who has prepared the accounts for that year, then this period of 3 months may not be material. On the other hand, the author has experienced businesses with accounts of up to 15 months in arrear, and if a purchaser is unaware of the elementary procedures to apply to calculate an estimation of profit, he may have wasted his energies in his researches into the accounts by having to accept the word of a vendor in respect of the current period. If this period relates to several months, then a trend may have evolved to give an entirely new perspective to the venture.

If the accounts of the current period are more than a year in arrear, the best advice to a purchaser must be for him to insist on the accounts being prepared for the year before taking any further interest in the business. If the period involved is under 12 months, then ideally the vendor should arrange for the information to be prepared or, alternatively, ask the permission of the vendor for the purchaser's own accountant to be employed, perhaps sharing the cost between the two parties. Even so, if one of the two alternatives is accepted, it must be realized that by the time the accountant has ruled off the books and prepared accounts a further month may have elapsed, and the same problem will apply in respect of the subsequent period, and to this extent be no further forward.

A detailed programme of procedure in the event of the vendor maintaining a cash book recording his sales and expenses must be, first, to confirm its authenticity by checking that all bank items shown in the cash book are reflected in the statements as supplied by the bank. This is most important as it requires no great skill to prepare a cash book showing fictitious entries. To verify the cash book, check that all takings shown as such, subject only to cash retained to pay petty expenses and wages, are recorded in the bank statements by using a mark to denote they have been traced. When this has been completed for the whole of the current period, again go through both the cash book and bank statements, seeking explanations from the vendor of receipts which appear in one and not the other. Of the two, pay particular attention to sales shown as banked in the cash book, but which do not appear in the bank statements. They could be dummy entries for the purpose of bolstering turnover.

With regard to payments represented by cheques drawn in favour of suppliers, etc., confirm that all entries in the cash book also appear in the bank statements, again noting payments shown in one and not the other. Conversely to the foregoing paragraph, the payments to be particularly noted are those which reflect in the statements but not the cash book. If the cheques concerned relate to a business expense, its omission from the cash book could be an attempt to understate expenditure and thus unfairly increase profit.

If every entry in the cash book reconciles itself with a corresponding entry in the bank statements, you may assume the cash book is in order.

If this is so, note the total sales and expenses for the current period, analysing the latter between purchases of goods for resale and other expenses, then comparing them with the corresponding information of the same period of the previous year to establish the approximate current trading position.

Another interesting exercise is to calculate the theoretical expenditure on the purchase of goods for resale in respect of the current period by using the turnover achieved during the same period and the historical average gross profit percentage of the business.

First calculate the gross profit on turnover by

$$\frac{\text{Percentage gross profit}}{100} \times \frac{\text{Turnover}}{1} = \text{Gross profit}$$

and then deduct the gross profit from turnover to arrive at the estimated cost of the goods sold. This total should favourably compare with the expenditure on purchases as extracted from the cash book for the current period. If the total of the actual cheques drawn in favour of suppliers is substantially less than the cost of goods sold, it may be due to:

1 The vendor purchasing at keener prices
2 A reduction in level of stock.
3 Or as is more likely the total liabilities of the business have increased.

Also note in the cash book whether regular recurring expenses, such as rent (usually quarterly), electricity and gas (quarterly), general and water rates (half yearly), have been paid on time. If not, this may be a further indication that liabilities have increased.

If the vendor does not maintain a cash book, it is possible to establish similar but not so reliable information, as already indicated earlier in the chapter, for comparative purposes by using the bank statements of the business. Analyse the receipts shown on the statements between sales and other bankings of a non-trading nature, e.g. the sale of a motor car, with the aid of the bank pay-in slips. Similarly, analyse the payments side of the statements between goods for resale and other business expenses by using the returned cheques. Extract the same information in respect of the corresponding period of the previous year to complete the exercise.

From the chapters dealing with accounts you will have gathered that, to obtain accurate gross and net profit figures, it is necessary to evaluate stock. A purchaser may have neither the time nor the inclination to undertake a thorough stock valuation at this stage, bearing in mind that the task will also have to be undertaken on day of takeover, and therefore make unnecessary duplication. It is sometimes found, however, that a comparatively few items of stock account for a large percentage of the total, and by selecting, counting and valuing the major items a guide to the stock level can be ascertained, by comparing this total with the total of the same items of the previous inventory.

If the approximate stock can be ascertained by this method, the necessary information will be available to prepare a trading account, and therefore to ascertain the gross profit. Ideally, the gross profit percentage should be calculated both for the current period and for the corresponding period of the previous year for comparison purposes, as this is the only method which reliably indicates whether the turnover for the current period has been achieved at standard prices. If in real terms a decline in trade has set in during the current period,

5

it is possible over the short term to maintain or even increase turn-over artificially by selling at lower prices at the expense of reduced gross margins and lower stock levels.

Do not calculate sales for part of the current period and assume the same level of turnover applies to the whole. The period selected may be unrepresentative of the whole, as it may be the busy or slack time of the year for that particular trade.

All this may seem unnecessary, but it is surprising how a shopping precinct can alter in a relatively short period of time, especially if a local authority in endeavouring to improve the flow of traffic intro-duces parking meters, clearways, yellow band areas, pedestrian guard rails and subways. The author is aware of an excellent shopping centre being reduced to average in the space of 6 months by the erection of pavement guard rails and only granting access from one side of the shopping parade to the other by a pedestrian bridge.

CHAPTER II

Valuing a Business

Referring again to the details of a business as supplied by a business transfer agent, the circular may show the selling price expressed as or similar to £3,750 s.a.v. To repeat what is perhaps the obvious, this means the vendor is asking £3,750 for the fixed assets of the business including its goodwill and leasehold interest, together with a sum for the stock which will be additional to the £3,750 depending on its value at the time of takeover. The value of the fixed assets will be an inclusive figure, and there will be no attempt on the part of the vendor to break the price down between the various assets offered for sale. It is therefore in the interests of a purchaser to value each asset and ascertain the sum total of them as a comparison between this value and the asking price to form the basis of subsequent negotiation if the two values should be unrelated.

An attempt will now be made to explain how an asset valuation may be achieved. Although the most satisfactory method of buying a business is only to purchase the fixed assets, reference will also be made to certain current assets and liabilities in the event of the purchaser having to acquire the issued share capital of a limited company, where the vendor has made it a condition of sale for the transfer to be effected in this manner.

Potential

The value to place on the potential of a business can be dealt with simply. Unless the potential is obvious and imminent, as, for example, nearly completed blocks of flats being erected opposite a coin operated launderette, then disregard it altogether and value the prospects at nil. If there are apparent factors which will in the near future improve the trade of a business, then by all means allow a price in the valuation for them, but overgenerosity is not necessary.

The reason for this view is, if the prospects were so golden and imminent the vendor would undoubtedly postpone sale until his business was receiving the benefit of them, and they in turn would reflect themselves in the accounts by showing increasing turnover and profit. If the potential is there, it will only be realized through the hard work of the purchaser and the reward therefore should be his.

As a further example of potential, one would normally associate a petrol filling station located in a traffic congested urban main road with being a good site. In practice, so far as concerns the sale of petrol, the performance of this type of garage is usually poor. A motorist is reluctant to lose his place in a stream of traffic to fill up with petrol due to the difficulties of filtering back onto the road. The long term prospects of this garage may be the building of a bypass on the outskirts of town to take the flow of through traffic and thus eliminate the congestion in the town centre, enabling motorists to drive in and out of the garage more easily.

The opposite effect is sometimes achieved by the installation of traffic lights in the vicinity of a garage.

Goodwill

It would be too easy when considering the value of goodwill to state it is the price a willing buyer is prepared to pay a willing seller. There are many ways of valuing goodwill, but the method which is generally most acceptable to both buyer and seller at this level of negotiating the transfer of a business is to value it at the rate of between one to three times the average annual adjusted net profit of the business over the most recent period of between 2 and 5 years, or all of the period if the business was established within this period. Adjusted net profit means the net profit after allowing for factors, if any, which either an average proprietor would not accept as businesslike, or the inevitable happening of an event beyond control which can be foreseen and evaluated. The deduction of a salary from profits in lieu of a manager (if one has not been previously employed), or the deduction of a future increase in rent would be examples of such an adjustment. An example of an adjustment to be added to net profit is where a wife or other relative is in receipt of a salary from the business which cannot be justified in terms of services rendered. Care should be taken for making an allowance in the value of goodwill for any factor which is already fully reflected in the net profit of the business: otherwise a purchaser may pay twice for the same privilege.

Lease

The only way of having a lease properly valued is by employing the services of a surveyor, familiar with the location of the shop and possessing knowledge of the local demand for the type of property, allowing for the standard of accommodation above the shop area. With these considerations in mind, a surveyor generally makes use of calculating tables for valuation purposes, which basically assume that property values will continue to increase at a fixed rate each year.

To a purchaser lacking this specialized knowledge, but with experience of assessing shop rentals, a rule of thumb method for valuing a lease without a rent revision clause contained therein is to calculate two-fifths of the difference between the current rental and the rent payable under the lease, assuming the former is of a higher value than the latter, and multiplying this sum by the number of years remaining under the lease. In the unlikely event of the rent payable under the lease exceeding the current market value, unless there are imminent profitable development possibilities the value of the lease must be regarded as nil. It should be noted, however, that when a lease is separately valued the multiplying factor as referred to when considering the value of goodwill should be at a reduced level, otherwise an element of duplication in the value of goodwill may arise.

Fixtures and Fittings

It is recommended that the written-down value of fixtures and fittings, or any other wasting asset as appearing in a balance sheet, be ignored as there is little, if any, consistency between proprietors in the rate of depreciation applied to similar classes of assets. In addition, if the vendor had decided to sell one or more years previously, he may have revalued his assets on a 'going concern' basis, which means that depreciation previously provided is partly or wholly written back to increase the balance sheet value of the assets and thus justify a higher asking price.

A formula for assessing the average age of fixed assets was shown earlier in the book, and by using the principle together with a realistic rate for depreciation the written-down value of the assets may be recalculated to give an indication of the price to offer for them.

The life of fixtures and fittings usually associated with those as used in retailing is 12 to 15 years, making the annual rate for depreciation approximately $7\frac{1}{2}$ per cent by the straight line method. To recalculate the written-down value, take the gross cost of the asset as shown in the balance sheet and deduct therefrom, using the straight line method, $7\frac{1}{2}$ per cent per annum for each year the asset has been owned by the business as computed on the average life basis. The result will be an indication of its market value.

If an asset has been revalued on a 'going concern' basis, this will be indicated on the balance sheet by the use of the words, or an expression similar to, 'as revalued' appearing immediately after the asset in question. If no revaluation has taken place, the words 'at cost' will be shown after the asset. In the event of an asset revaluation having taken place, it will be possible to ascertain the cost by working backwards year by year from the most recent balance sheet until finding the first balance sheet noting 'at cost' against the asset. The gross cost on this balance sheet should be used for your calculation after adding thereto the cost of additions to the asset in subsequent years to date, which will be shown as 'additions, at cost'. An example of the recalculation is shown later in the chapter under the calculation for valuing a business.

When vendor and purchaser have finally agreed between them a price on which to complete the transaction, the price may again be an inclusive figure covering all the assets. For the purpose of the preparation of the vending agreement it will be necessary for the solicitor to split the agreed price between the freehold/leasehold and goodwill on the one hand and the remaining assets on the other for stamp duty purposes, the rates of which have already been mentioned. As stamp duty is only payable on the value of the freehold/leasehold and goodwill, there is a tendency for the purchaser to value these assets as low a possible, and for the vendor to value the same group of assets as high as possible for his own personal income tax purposes. Having reached this advanced stage, it is in the interests of both parties to compromise on this point and the purchaser will be assisted when expressing his views by his detailed asset valuation.

Other fixed assets, with the exception of those already mentioned and motor vehicles, should be dealt with in the same manner as provided under the heading of fixtures and fittings.

Motor Vehicle

If a motor vehicle is to form part of the transaction, a valuation can be readily ascertained from a garage or from one of the motoring journals.

Stock

One of the reasons previously mentioned for the sale of a business was the possibility of the vendor being overstocked and having insufficient finance to buy new. It is a useful calculation, therefore, to ascertain the value of stock the vendor is holding in terms of selling prices, and translating this information into how long it will take to sell under normal conditions. For an example, the closing stock and gross profit margin as shown in the trading account in Chapter 5 are used (G.P. = gross profit):

$$\left(\frac{\text{Rate of G.P.}(\%)}{100 - \text{Rate of G.P.}(\%)} \times \frac{\text{Value of stock}}{1} \right) + \text{Value of stock}$$
$$= \text{Selling price of stock}$$

$$\left(\frac{24 \cdot 3}{100 - 24 \cdot 3} \times \frac{3626}{1} \right) + 3626 = \text{Selling price}$$

$$\left(\frac{24 \cdot 3}{75 \cdot 7} \times \frac{3626}{1} \right) + 3626 = \text{Selling price}$$

$$1164 + 3626 = £4,800 \text{ approx.}$$

Assuming the closing stock as shown in the balance sheet of £3,626 is eventually sold at an average gross profit of 24·3 per cent to conform with the historical experience of the business, it will realize £4,800. Continuing with the calculation, the annual turnover is at the level of £19,726; therefore, to ascertain the sales/stock ratio divide £4,800 by the annual turnover to equal 0·24 of a year, which again may be expressed in a more familiar way of 3 months, usually considered to be a reasonable stock level. If the calculation shows the stock will take 6 months or more to dispose of, it will suggest the vendor is overstocked and point towards the possibility of the business holding an unreasonably high percentage of old and un-saleable lines, which any vendor would be more than pleased to sell at cost price to enable him to recover his money in full.

Fortunately, the average retailer is not renowned for spending large sums of money on maintenance and heating of his stock room, which generally makes old stock self-apparent by the appearance and con-dition of the packaging material. Inspect the stockroom, and pay particular attention to any stock stored in the awkward corners, as the new and fast moving lines are often stored in the accessible areas to facilitate easy replacement for shop display purposes.

It will serve no useful purpose to count stock at this stage as the relevant time will be the day of takeover, but no harm is done by isolating in advance the older stock which may be below par value.

It is recommended that on the day of transfer of a business the purchaser makes it a condition for the stock to be counted and evaluated by an independent valuer, as so often it is found that the fees charged are more than offset by savings achieved resulting from the professional valuation. It is advisable for both the vendor and purchaser to attend the valuation, and any points noted regarding suspect stock by the latter during his preliminary survey of the stock should be drawn to the attention of the valuer before he commences his duties.

If, for financial or other reasons, it is not possible for a profess-ional valuer to be employed, the duties involved in valuing stock are tabulated as follows:

1 The stock must be counted systematically to ensure no part of it is recorded twice. As an aid to reduce the possibility of this happening, use chalk to suitably mark the stock or shelving on which it is stored to denote it has been counted. Ignore any pressures designed to hasten the physical counting.

2 Make suitable notes on the stock sheets against the quantities covering items which are damaged or old, and those which will not command full selling price, for further reference later when the stock is valued.

3 To avoid the possibility of any subsequent dispute arising after the stock has been counted, both parties should initial each stock sheet to denote their agreement with the quantities as recorded. Furthermore, it should also be agreed that any objections regarding quantities made after the counting has been completed cannot be considered.

When the stock has been counted, the next stage must be to price each item with the aid of purchase invoices. It is usually found necessary to have at least the most recent 12 months' purchase invoices available before commencing the procedure which is again tabulated:

1 The pricing of stock should not be attempted by taking an item from the stock sheets and referring to the supplier's invoice, as there is no guarantee that the current price will be extracted for evaluation purposes. The most satisfactory method is to consecutively go through the invoices in the files, from the most recent invoice and working backwards. This method of valuation known as the 'first in – first out' method will ensure that, whenever the first invoice is found relating to goods also appearing in the stock sheets, the price will be the most recent one at which the vendor has purchased. The valuation of stock by the 'first in – first out' method is usually considered to be the fairest to both parties concerned.

Stocks should never be valued by using manufacturers' or wholesalers' price lists, the two most relevant reasons for this being:

a A recent price increase may have been imposed and reflected in the price lists which were printed subsequent to the last purchase made by the vendor.

b The vendor may have received a special price or quantity discount which will only become apparent by reference to an invoice.

2 When inspecting an invoice, note the name of the supplier, the description of goods and the date of the invoice: the latter to ensure it is current. Compare the description of the goods with those on the stock sheets to trace if any of that particular stock is held. If stock is held, record full details of the price against the item on the stock sheet, paying particular attention to see if the price quoted is for one or for a quantity, i.e. 30*s* each or 30*s* per dozen. In addition, also record on the stock sheet any trade discount allowed to the vendor which may not be self-apparent, as it may be shown by way of a

deduction on the invoice by appearing at the foot of it to reduce the gross cost. If the invoice relates to several items, and the trade discount is shown as just mentioned, the discount will equally apply to all the purchases shown on the invoice and the items noted accordingly. An example of an item of stock when priced may be:

154 Shirts, collar attached, white 270*s* per doz. less 10%

C. Parker & Co. Ltd.

The effective net price is therefore 243*s* per dozen.

In certain trades it is customary for the manufacturer to invoice the retailer for his purchases at the recommended retailers' selling prices and to allow him his margin by deducting the trade discount therefor. This again emphasizes the importance of looking for trade discounts on an invoice, otherwise the vendor will be realizing his stock at selling prices.

3 If the quantity of an item of stock, as counted and recorded on the stock sheets, is greater than the quantity shown on the most recent purchase invoice, this must indicate that part of the stock is older and at least a second invoice is involved. Under these circumstances, record the price in the normal way but also show the quantity of stock to which the price relates. The subsequent invoice for the same goods must be used for pricing the outstanding unpriced balance of stock. As a factual example, assume 500 ties are held in stock and the most recent invoice was for 300 ties at 5*s* 6*d* each, then note the information against the 500 ties. The previous purchase was 2 months earlier when 350 ties were purchased at 4*s* 6*d* each. The balance of the tie stock of 200 must, therefore, be valued at 4*s* 6*d* each. If all the ties are valued at 5*s* 6*d* each, the cost to the purchaser of the business would be £137 10*s* 0*d*, whereas the correct valuation should be £127 10*s* 0*d*, thus showing a saving of £10. This is perhaps not a great saving, but if multiplied by other items which may arise during stock valuation affected by the same principle, a substantial saving could be achieved. In practice, it is sometimes found that four or more invoices may be necessary to value some items of stock.

4 The position must be reached when systematically inspecting invoices where the date of the first invoice in respect of an unpriced item of stock must, out of necessity, earmark the item as being old. The type of trade of the business is the material factor in the selection

of the date, as may be shown by an example of an invoice indicating the stock to be 6 months' old. If the item was for refrigerators, then the age is not so important as it would be in the case of the purchase of ladies' fashion wear.

Once a purchaser has established in his mind the condition and age of stock he will accept and pay for in full he should not be deterred from his policy and must negotiate accordingly, as there can be no suggestion of a purchaser paying for the mistakes of the vendor. Therefore, with regard to stock which for any reason is substandard, do not hesitate to value the items at nil or, at best, at a value not exceeding the selling price for disposal during a sale after allowing for a gross profit margin. If the stock is valued at a price in excess of the subsequent selling value, a loss will be incurred to be suffered by the purchaser. If the vendor objects to this method being applied, it can always be suggested to him that he may continue his ownership of the substandard stock for his disposal on the best terms he is able to negotiate with a third party.

An alternative method to the one mentioned above, in the event of both parties failing to agree on a valuation for shop-soiled or old stock, is for the stock to be omitted from the valuation for subsequent sale by the purchaser on behalf of the vendor at the best possible prices, the full proceeds of which, less an agreed commission, to be remitted to the vendor.

5 Allow in the pricing for any writing-off, either wholly or partially, which may be necessary to conform with the notes on the stock sheets made at the time of the physical stocktaking in the manner referred to in item (4) above.

6 If the stock consists of products which require after-sales service, i.e. electrical goods, the purchaser should satisfy himself that the manufacturers are still in existence, having regard to the fact that the purchase of spares will be necessary. Any products held in stock originating from a manufacturer no longer in business must be suspect.

7 When the stock has been priced with invoices for the selected period the stock which remains unpriced may be either old stock (referred to in (4) above), or lines obtained from an irregular source of supply, possibly a job lot paid for in cash. The pricing of stock of this nature

must be by negotiation, having regard to whatever supporting evidence is made available by the vendor, again bearing in mind the value must not exceed the estimated selling price.

8 When the stock has been fully priced in accordance with the foregoing, the final procedure is to evaluate each item of stock by multiplying the price as extracted from the invoice, or as otherwise negotiated, by the quantity recorded on the stock sheet, leaving only the total column to be added up. This total will represent the liability of the purchaser for the stock.

Sundry Debtors

The valuation of sundry debtors does not usually present a problem in the case of a retail business as sales are generally made on a cash basis. However, the vendor may have a few regular customers to whom he permits a credit account, and if any debts are in existence at the date of transfer which are not to form part of the sale the usual arrangement is for the purchaser to remit the proceeds when received from the credit customers direct to the vendor, less an agreed handling commission.

If special factors exist where it is necessary for the purchaser to buy the debtors for his own account as, for example, if the vendor is emigrating, thus involving him in an application under the exchange control regulations to remit his capital abroad, the following procedure should be followed for the valuation of the debtor balances:

1 Inspect at date of transfer every unpaid credit account in the sales ledger and note the period of time it has remained outstanding.

2 If a previous credit sale is shown on the account, together with the receipt of a cheque in settlement thereof, calculate the period of credit usually taken by the customer and compare this period with the period of the unpaid balance, noting if the period is in excess of the normal period of credit usually taken by the customer.

3 List the outstanding accounts on analysis paper under separate headings as follows:

Total	I *Month*	2–3 *Months*	4–6 *Months*	7–12 *Months*	12 *Months and over*

The outstanding amount due from each debtor should be listed in the total column and again listed under the relevant analysis column, depending on the time the account has remained unpaid. When all balances have been listed, total each column and ensure that the total column equals the sum total of the analysis columns. A suggested price structure to pay the vendor for the debtors is:

Debts of under a month	Pay in full
Debts of between 2–3 months outstanding	Deduct 20% of the total in anticipation of a few bad debts arising
Debts of between 4–6 months outstanding	Deduct 40% of the total
Debts of between 7–12 months outstanding	Deduct 80% of the total

All balances outstanding for a period in excess of 12 months should be regarded as bad debts and valued at nil.

In certain trades where sales by hire purchase form a regular feature of business, the problem may arise between vendor and purchaser as to how the outstanding hire purchase agreements may best be dealt with. If the retailer has an arrangement with a finance company for them to finance all hire purchase transactions, then no accounting problems will arise for the purchaser, other than to continue to receive the monthly repayments from customers and remit the proceeds to the finance house. There is a non-accounting problem, however, which may concern a purchaser.

To give the historical background, during the mid-1960's many finance companies either went into liquidation or suffered severe losses through bad debts following the halcyon days of the late 1950's and early 1960's when there was fierce competition between them to obtain business, some of which was achieved regardless of cost or commercial prudence. As a result of this experience, finance companies have recently endeavoured to obtain a written guarantee from retailers to indemnify themselves against bad debts arising from business introduced by the retailers, the purpose being to encourage a degree of customer selectivity on the part of retailers before making a sale. When a vendor has the support of finance houses, therefore, a purchaser or his solicitor should write to all finance houses with whom the vendor has had dealings enquiring if such a guarantee is in existence and, if so, whether it was given in the name of the vendor or his business. If the indemnity is the responsibility of the vendor, no problem arises for the purchaser other than to refer in the agreement for sale of the businesss that no assignment of the contingent liability is implied. If the undertaking was made on behalf of the business, any liability arising therefrom will accrue to the purchaser and the finance house should be requested for a statement showing whether a liability has arisen under the guarantee as at the date of transfer. If a liability has arisen, the position must be considered carefully in the light of the information supplied.

By virtue of the profitable nature of hire purchase business it occasionally happens that a vendor has in the past financed with his own money certain hire purchase transactions by selecting for his purpose sales made to customers in the higher income groups, leaving a hire purchase company to finance the remainder. If this position exists in the business in which a purchaser is interested, apply the procedure referred to in an earlier paragraph by listing and analysing the outstanding hire purchase accounts and paying for them accordingly. This procedure assumes that the vendor wishes to sell the outstanding hire purchase accounts at date of sale; otherwise continue to collect the repayments for the vendor and remit the proceeds to him, again after deducting an agreed handling commission.

Cash at Bank and in Hand

It is the custom on the sale of a business for the vendor to retain the cash at bank and in hand by transferring the balances to his own private account immediately prior to transfer.

You should be reminded, however, that buying the bank and cash balances may occasionally be to the advantage of a purchaser for a reason which is perhaps best explained by the following example. Assume the value of a business has been agreed by the two parties at £5,000, which sum excludes a balance at bank of £1,000 to be retained by the vendor; also assume the purchaser anticipates he will only be able to negotiate from his bank a loan to cover the capital cost of the business, the bank being unwilling to extend the facility to provide for working capital on the same principle as a building society will advance money to buy the house, but not to pay for the rates. By renegotiating with the vendor to include the bank balance with the other assets for sale at £6,000 (£5,000 plus balance at bank of £1,000) the purchaser may, with care, express to his bank the cost of the business as being £6,000. If the bank advances the difference between the capital available by the purchaser and the cost of £6,000, the purchaser will then have £1,000 in the business for his use as working capital. The purchaser must satisfy himself that the money is not withdrawn from the business by the vendor before transfer, and should forward a new mandate to the bank as soon after transfer as possible.

Cash Paid in Advance

In certain trades it is customary to accept from customers cash in advance of sale in the form of deposits on goods or savings for a Christmas club run by the proprietor to be exchanged for goods later in the year. In the case of a Christmas club, it is possible for a considerable sum of money to accumulate in a business and a purchaser should ascertain whether such a club is in existence and, if so, arrange for the balances to be transferred to himself. Failing the discovery of such a club, a purchaser will be in a difficult position during the following pre-Christmas period when customers will expect the goods which they have saved up for, leaving the purchaser either to claim that the savings given to the vendor is of no concern to him and suffer the consequent bad will, or, alternatively, maintain happy customer relations by fulfilling all obligations at his own expense.

Liabilities

Another example of when it can be an advantage to buy the current assets and liabilities of a business is in the case of a limited company with tax losses, as it is possible to offset them against future profits and thus reduce future tax liabilities to the extent of the tax losses. To safeguard the availability of tax losses, it is necessary for the purchaser to acquire the issued share capital from the vendor, to establish to the satisfaction of the Inland Revenue that continuity of trade is maintained within the meaning of corporation tax legislation.

To ensure as far as possible the accuracy of the liabilities, a purchaser should see at least the current monthly statements rendered by the larger suppliers and reconcile them with their respective accounts in the bought ledger of the vendor. If the balance in the bought ledger is less than that as shown on the supplier's statement, it may indicate the vendor has made purchases and has either accidentally mislaid or deliberately suppressed invoices, and copies of the missing invoices should be obtained from the respective supplier to establish whether or not they are a liability of the company. If the vendor cannot produce statements from the larger suppliers, the suppliers should be asked to forward an up-to-date copy, preferably addressed direct to the purchaser or his accountant. The smaller bought ledger accounts should be verified with whatever statements are available, and ideally copies requested for the unverified balances, but in view of the time factor this may not always be possible.

Reference has already been made to the possibility of withholding part of the purchase price from the vendor until the debtors have been realized and the liabilities correctly established.

Making a Valuation

It is a near impossibility to value a hypothetical business. However, an attempt will be made to value the business represented by the accounts detailed in Chapter 5 of the sole trader to show the basic principles involved. It is necessary to make assumptions and the following will apply.

A Sole Trader (Chapter 5)
1 On the 1st January following the 31st December of the financial year end the vendor entered into a new lease at a current market rental of £650 per annum, making the value of his interest in the leasehold a nominal one of £200.
2 The vendor decides to retain the car, cash in hand and balance at bank, and agrees that the sundry debtors and liabilities will also not form part of the sale.
3 The private living expenses of the vendor charged to the business are to the extent as shown in the following calculation; likewise are the expenses for the private use of the motor car.

4 The salary of a manager, if appointed, would cost the business an additional £1,000 per annum.

5 The wage paid to the wife is a justifiable business expense as she is employed in the business to the full extent of the wage paid.

6 The valuation for goodwill is agreed to be based at the rate of $2\frac{1}{4}$ times of the adjusted net profit for the year.

7 It is also agreed that the proper charge for depreciation of fixtures and fittings should be $7\frac{1}{2}$ per cent straight line method per annum and not at the rate of 5 per cent per annum as reflected in the accounts.

Calculation

	£	£	£
Net profit as per accounts		1,683	
Add : Private expenses charged to the business :			
Rental		160	
General and water rates		80	
Lighting and heating		40	
Telephone		15	
Motor expenses		110	
Motor depreciation		100	
		2,188	
Less : Salary of manager	1,000		
Increased rental	100	1,100	
Adjust net profit		£1,088	
Value of Goodwill—$2\frac{1}{4}$ times thereof			2,450
Value of Lease			200
Value of fixtures and fittings, Cost (9 years old—average life basis)	1,100		
Less : Depreciation £1,100 at $7\frac{1}{2}$% × 9	740		360
Asset valuation			£3,010

In practice, the vendor may be asking £3,150 for his business; the purchaser may offer £2,850 and a compromise be reached at £3,000 to which must be added the value of stock, calculated in accordance with the method shown earlier in this chapter.

6

CHAPTER 12

General

The concern of the previous chapters has been to establish broad principles rather than matters of detail, but as certain trades are affected by special features it is now necessary to refer to the more important of them in addition to briefly mentioning the law as affecting clauses in restraint of trade.

Sub-Post Office

If negotiations are finalized with a proprietor who is also a sub-postmaster, then it is advisable for the purchaser to incorporate in the agreement for sale provision covering either an adjustment to the purchase price or cancellation of the agreement if the Post Office terminates its contract for the site of the business to be a sub-Post Office.

Technically the appointment of a sub-postmaster is a personal one and not an arrangement entered into with a business; therefore, when a sub-postmaster intends to dispose of his business, he must give the Post Office 3 months' notice to terminate his agreement as sub-postmaster. The Post Office, in accordance with standing regulations, must then advertise the vacancy of sub-postmaster for a period of 3 weeks, and interested persons may apply for the position by completing an application form designed for the purpose. All applicants are considered and the shortlisted candidates are invited to attend an interview. In addition to the usual assessment of character the Post Office must also consider the location of the premises available by each applicant and the facilities provided before a final selection can be made.

Although the Post Office insist that the replacement of a retiring sub-postmaster is competitively made, the prospective purchaser of a business with an established sub-Post Office has practical advantages which the Area Postmaster cannot ignore. The established sub-Post

Office will be located in premises already well known to local inhabitants and will have the necessary facilities to comply with the requirements of the Post Office, especially as regards security of the premises where anti-burglar devices, safes, etc. can be expensive items to install. In addition, the Post Office cannot ignore the time factor involved by appointing a sub-postmaster with an alternative site, by virtue of the delay in obtaining planning permission and carrying out the necessary alteration to the premises, thus resulting in inconvenience to the public.

It is unusual, therefore, for a purchaser of an established sub-Post Office to be unsuccessful in his application even if he cannot substantiate previous experience of the duties involved. The Post Office will arrange for the successful applicant to attend a counter course and, although no remuneration is paid during the period of training, neither will a charge be made. Following the period of training the purchaser will also have the assistance of an experienced Post Office employee for a period of 2 to 3 weeks after purchase to act in an advisory capacity and to make sure the duties are carried out properly. Before an agreement is formally offered by the Post Office the successful applicant must be fidelity bonded, which will necessitate extensive enquiries being made with his previous employers concerning character and honesty. The contract with the Post Office will be subject, as already indicated, to 3 months' notice of termination by either side.

If running a sub-Post Office appeals to you, but you lack courage at the thought of mastering the many and varied forms and duties to be dealt with, then do not lose interest on this account as the training programme is designed for people like you. The Post Office will not leave anyone in charge of a sub-Post Office unless they are fully satisfied the duties will be attended to properly. After all, it is their money you will be playing with.

Public House and Other Business Requiring a Liquor Licence

A liquor licence is another example of a right being awarded to an individual as opposed to a business; therefore, a purchaser of a business requiring a liquor licence will have to take the necessary steps to obtain one in his own name.

The application must be submitted to the local Licencing Justices, whose address can be obtained from any Post Office. The application will be referred by the Licencing Officer to the Police for their investigation, which will mainly cover the character of the applicant to ensure that he is a suitable and responsible person to whom such a licence can be granted.

Sale of Tobacco

All that is necessary to obtain a tobacco licence is to submit an application to the local Police. If the vendor had a licence to sell tobacco, then it can usually be regarded as a mere formality for the purchaser to be granted one also.

Garages

Exaggerated claims are sometimes made by vendors of garages concerning the annual rate of petrol and diesel oil sold by their station. The information can be verified, however, by writing to the petroleum company from whom the vendor obtains his supplies for details of the annual gallonage sold by them to the vendor.

Earlier in the book a chapter was devoted to the various methods of obtaining finance. It is appropriate to mention under this heading that petroleum companies also offer finance if the garage in question is tied to the company or in exchange for a tie. Since the Monopolies Commission Report on the petroleum company–garage relationship, the duration of a tie is now usually limited to 7 years, unless finance is made available by the petroleum company, in which event it may be for a longer period. If this seems excessive, it must be appreciated that it is only reasonable for a petroleum company to receive benefit by securing outlets for its products in exchange for a loan facility.

It is not possible to quote the extent of loan finance available from the many petroleum companies, as it must vary depending on how badly they require the site offered at that moment in time, but a 50 per cent advance is commonplace, and may be higher in the case of an applicant who is able to show a successful record of garage/filling station experience, or if the company will be gaining what they consider to be a valuable new outlet.

Chemists

It is not necessary to be a qualified pharmacist to own a chemist shop, but one must be employed to dispense prescriptions and sell drugs. The number of pharmacists available for employment is restricted; therefore a competitive salary must be offered to attract applications for the position.

Selling Concessions and Agencies

A prospective purchaser should enquire whether a business with selling concessions and other forms of selling agency derives the benefit therefrom through arrangements made in the name of the vendor or his business. If the former, the agreements are of a personal nature and a purchaser should ensure that the benefits will be assigned to himself on completion of sale.

Clause of Restraint of Trade

It has firmly been established at law on many occasions that every man is entitled to earn his daily bread by any legal means open to him, including using his skills in a trade in which he is able to make the best use of them to his personal advantage.

The interpretation of the foregoing maxim within the context of this book is that, unless provision is made to the contrary, there is no reason why a vendor of a business should not acquire other premises in close vicinity to the business he sold, and again commence to employ his experience in the same trade. If this should happen the vendor may regain, over a period of time, many of his old customers and give the purchaser of his previous business a sickly feeling as the latter sees his capital investment, trade and profit melt away.

It is of the utmost importance in the vending agreement, therefore, that the solicitor representing the purchaser should insert a suitable clause of restraint of trade. Unless the consideration paid to the vendor is greatly in excess of the amount usually associated with the sale of a business, for such a clause to be enforceable at law it must not prohibit the vendor from working for all future time, or even prohibit him from seeking employment in or buying another business in the same trade as the one he disposed of, but it will offer protection against the vendor from using his knowledge of the trade in any way within such a radius as to affect his old business.

It is also advisable to seek the advice of a solicitor regarding the insertion of a restraint clause in the contract of employment of a manager, or other senior person, whom you may appoint. A clause in restraint of trade in the contract of an employee will only be able to restrict his future earning activities to a very limited degree, but the clause may afford some safeguard if, later, the employee works for a competitor or if he establishes a business on his own account in the same trade.

Conclusion

If the only achievement of this book has been to make its reader fully aware of the importance of professional advice, then it will have achieved one of its main objects. If, on the other hand, you are left with the feeling: How can anyone possibly risk money by buying a business?, the reader must be reminded that the majority of businesses are sold without any undue problems arising and the result is a comfortable livelihood for the new owner. It is only in the minority of cases that there is danger of a partial or total loss of capital, and it is this type of business which the public must be protected against as there are no second chances for the unfortunate buyers concerned.

This is not to be associated with the feeling which most people have after moving into a new house when minor faults become apparent which were not noticed at the time of survey. This may happen after buying a business and, if so, accept it philosophically and consider, one day you may be a seller too. . . .

Part two – Running a Business

CHAPTER 13

Retailing

The remaining chapters will be concerned with the running of a business on the assumption that the new proprietor has had no previous experience in the field. On this understanding a new proprietor may wish, during the early weeks of his ownership, to consider the policy of conducting the business in the same way as it was conducted by his predecessor on the basis that during the short term he should achieve the same results as the vendor. By this is meant that if a new proprietor continues to buy and sell identical goods at the same prices, using the same suppliers and employing the same assistants, he should make the same rate of profit while gaining time to obtain the necessary experience and know-how of the trade to enable new policies to be formulated which, when implemented, will stand a much better chance of success. There is nothing difficult about making a change; the real problem arises when a new policy has again to be altered if it should prove to be unsuccessful.

There are a few basic rules which have stood the test of time and they are, therefore, worth repeating.

Pricing

Never consistently sell too many goods at prices which are too low. There is nothing particularly clever about doing this, as turnover can easily be substantially increased by selling goods at cost prices, to take an extreme example. Against this it can truthfully be argued that the supermarket attracts custom by price cutting, but two points should not be overlooked. First, a supermarket only cuts prices on perhaps a dozen items out of a range of two to three thousand lines, depending on the floor area available for display purposes at the shop. Second, even when prices are cut, the reduction is usually made in conjunction with and at the expense of a manufacturer, who occasionally quotes at special prices either to reduce his stock or to reduce his unit fixed overhead expenses by achieving an increased volume of production. A supermarket rarely sells at a price to show a return of less than its normal gross profit margin. A poundsworth of sales only equals a £1 note, and if it can be obtained by selling three articles at full price instead of four articles at a cut price, at worst you are possibly saving the employment of extra staff which would otherwise be necessary to cope with the additional volume of work. In any event, it does not necessarily mean that by cutting prices by 25 per cent the additional quantity will be sold to equal the cash value of the goods if they had been sold at full price.

Having said that, take advantage of a sales period to liquidate slow moving or overstocked lines to realize cash to finance the purchase of more popular and faster moving products. Also gain from the experience of supermarkets, who introduce special offers on only a few lines at a time in conjunction with making the offer at the expense of the supplier and not at your own whenever possible. Alternatively, many businesses successfully operate by buying out-of-season lines in bulk at cheaper prices (the question of adequate finance arises), or by buying cheaper imported quality goods, or goods specifically manufactured in Great Britain for a sale, as may be seen by the decline in the standards of quality of many goods sold during the winter and summer sales campaign periods.

A consistent changing sales policy on the lines as indicated adds interest to a business which invariably results in many shoppers making a habit of looking in the window—the first step towards them becoming regular customers.

Attention is drawn to the paragraph in the final chapter of the book dealing with the Trade Descriptions Act, 1968, certain sections of which must be considered before formulating a sales pricing policy.

Before finally leaving the subject of pricing some regard must be paid to retail price maintenance. Although, technically, retail price maintenance has ended under the provisions of the Resale Prices Act, 1964, a few companies are still able to impose retail selling prices on specified goods with the approval of the Restrictive Practices Court, founded under the terms of the Act, by substantiating to the satisfaction of that Court that one of the conditions for granting exemption is fulfilled in their particular circumstances.

The grounds for exemption are that to discard price maintenance will be detrimental to the interests of the public as consumers or users on account of the fact that:

1 The quality and number of varieties of particular goods will decline, or
2 The number of establishments selling the products will decline, or
3 Prices in the long run will increase, or
4 The after-sales service of goods requiring such service will cease or become more difficult, or
5 Goods will be sold under conditions injurious to health.

A company may also impose price maintenance if it has applied for exemption to the Restrictive Practices Court and is awaiting for the hearing of the case, or if the Court has decided against the company and it has lodged notice of appeal.

If, unwittingly, a retailer should reduce the price of one of the few products still subject to price maintenance below the manufacturer's recommended price, experience shows that the manufacturer will in the first place warn the offender, and if the retailer persists with the reduction, the manufacturer may then seek an injunction from a Civil Court restraining the retailer from so doing or, alternatively, withdraw supplies from him.

Assistants

There is nothing more certain to encourage regular customers than to consistently employ smart, obliging and polite assistants. Most people have had the unfortunate experience of entering a shop and being treated rudely or with a 'take it or leave it' attitude, with the result that the customer is reluctant to patronize the shop again. The public can be very demanding and it requires at times great will-power to maintain 'the customer is always right' attitude, but perseverance will in the long term pay handsome dividends.

Sales Promotion

A further aid to sales can be the introduction of trading stamps, provided an agency is established with one of the well known companies, preferably the largest company in the field. Trading stamp companies claim that an increase in turnover of 60 per cent can be achieved by the clever use of the media. Although the author is not aware of any increase to this extent through the use of trading stamps, he is aware of businesses who have achieved a permanent increase in turnover of 20 per cent.

A trading stamp company will only grant a sole concession to one business in any particular trade in a given area. The written agreement usually provides, however, that the arrangement can be terminated by 30 days' notice in writing by either party, which the stamp companies do not hesitate to do in the event of their entering into an arrangement with a multiple retailer servicing the same area as the existing concessionaire. The cost of trading stamps amounts to between $2\frac{1}{2}$ and $3\frac{1}{2}$ per cent of turnover, using single stamps, depending on the quantity of stamps purchased at a time.

One of the principal advantages of the use of trading stamps is during a special offer campaign where it is possible to offer double or treble stamps while maintaining standard prices. Treble stamps will only cost a maximum of an addition 7 per cent on turnover, a reduction which would be unacceptable to the public if the incentive was a straight 7 per cent discount off cash prices. The maximum number of stamps offered must depend on the average gross profit margin of the trade, but in any event the stamp supplier will not permit more than quadruple stamps to be given.

A summary of the Trading Stamps Act, 1964, is given in the final chapter.

Presentation

The sales presentation of products is another important factor, particularly the window display which psychologically seems to convey to the public how the business is conducted generally. Consider the window displays of shops with which you are familiar to confirm how true this is. A dusty looking display, which has obviously not been changed for ages, invariably reflects both on the character of the proprietor and the methods he employs to conduct his business. The converse is equally true of a business with a window display which is everchanging, clean and tidy, and is obviously eager to seek your custom.

To properly design and lay out a shop window display requires experience, and until this has been acquired consideration should be given to employing the services of a specialist firm of window dressers. They will change the window as often as you are prepared to pay for their services, which in the case of fashion wear should be frequently. Nothing is more contrived to make a shop ignored by the public than when they know from experience the goods on offer for sale and hence do not bother to look into the window.

While on the subject of window displays, many of the older premises have frontages which were designed for use in a different era, when little attention was paid to the profitable use of floor area. The cost of having a new shop front installed has been greatly reduced recently by the introduction of the semi-ready-made shop front unit, which is both quick and easy to erect while permitting the business to continue to trade as usual. A modern styled shop front has the dual purpose of allowing for a greater floor selling area within a shop and reducing the amount of stock needed to be tied up in a window display which may become shop-soiled through overexposure to the sun.

There are many trades making greater use of display stands by introducing full or partial customer self-service which in many cases are provided free of charge by the manufacturer. It was recently reported, for example, that one shop in every two in the grocery trade is now self-service. If the idea of a manufacturer's company-named display stand being on your premises does not appeal to you, then display units can be purchased comparatively cheaply to your own specification. The advantages of a self-service display area are:

1 It provides for a greater range of products to be within easy reach of the customer to stimulate impulse buying, and
2 It reduces the number of shop assistants required.

It must be noted, however, that the economies achieved be self-service are partially offset by losses through pilferage, which appear to account for between $2\frac{1}{2}$ and 4 per cent of turnover. It is perhaps a sad reflection on today's world, but supermarkets regard losses through pilferage in the same manner as they regard rent and other similar costs, that is, as an unavoidable expense.

CHAPTER 14

Buying

A great deal of attention is naturally paid to retailing, in consequence of which there is a tendency for buying to be regarded as of minor importance among the many functions necessary to run a business. Why this should be the author is not clear, as it has been his experience that a good buyer can contribute as much to the general prosperity of a business as can a good salesman. The duties of a salesman are trying at the best of times, but his task can be made easier if he is continually supported by being able to offer good products at the right prices at the right times.

To start with, continue to purchase your requirements from the same suppliers as used by the vendor to ensure that the quality of the products for sale is maintained. Before placing an order always refer to previous invoices from the same supplier and compare the price with the price of the current quotation, paying particular attention to the rate of trade discount, if any. If the price of the quotation is higher, ensure that the increase is a general one to the trade and not to you in particular. If the latter is applicable, satisfy yourself that the increase is justified and not simply a 'try-on' because of your being new to the trade. If a price increase is applied by the supplier and accepted, make a note for when the goods are received that the respective selling prices will have to be increased, otherwise the gross profit margin of the business will suffer in consequence.

Make a rule that all orders placed with suppliers are given or subsequently confirmed in writing. A favourite practice of the less reputable company is for them to fulfil an order in excess of the one received, especially if taken over the telephone, and invoice for the goods accordingly.

An essential aid to good buying is the maintenance of information in respect of each supplier. A suggestion towards this end is for the preparation of a file and a record card for every company from which purchases are made. The file may be used for holding correspondence to establish a case history of dealings with a particular supplier, and for the temporary filing of copy orders, advice notes and delivery notes pending the reconciliation of these documents with the invoices when received. Each supplier will draw attention to his own conditions of sale by usually printing them on the reverse side of the quotation, invoice or acceptance of order, and an effort should be made to read them as frequently the conditions reflect the business principles of the company concerned. An extract of the conditions may be written on the inside cover of the file, or possibly the same space used to attach an old document listing the conditions in detail.

With regard to the record card, an abbreviated history of business carried on with the company is all that is necessary. The date of each order placed, order number, a brief description of goods ordered, the price and date of delivery can be recorded as a ready means of access for information to assist when placing the subsequent order with the same supplier. Space can also be provided to record the total amount of the invoice when received to reduce the possibility of duplicating the payment of the account. In any event, no account should be paid unless the details of every invoice are previously confirmed with the quotation, order and delivery note, which, if they are in agreement therewith, may all be stapled to the invoice. If the supporting documents referred to are not available for any particular invoice, this may suggest that the goods have not been received due to the dispatch note having been addressed incorrectly. It is surprising how often this happens, especially if the manufacturer distributes his products by subcontracted transport.

Many proprietors seem to regard a sales representative as a nuisance, and perhaps he is if he continually calls during the busy periods of the week. The successful trader, however, does not regard him as such, but goes out of his way to know each representative by encouraging him to call on his slack days. Familiarize yourself with the products each representative offers, and consider carefully those which may usefully extend or improve your range, while at the same time retaining a moment for reflection to satisfy yourself fully that a product is marketable before placing an order. A trial order to test market reaction is sometimes indicated where doubt exists.

When assessing similar products made by differing manufacturers do not necessarily always compare then from the viewpoint of price, but also have regard to quality in relation to price. A buyer once estimated that one new product in every ten interested him, of which only a half were supported by an order, the question of price only playing a comparatively minor role in the final selection. This supports the view that one of the essential requirements of a skilful buyer is patience if a sense of proportion is to be retained.

Another advantage of encouraging representatives to call is that they are a ready source for the exchange of new ideas by virtue of their being in constant contact with other proprietors in the same trade. However clever you may be, there is always someone with an even better idea which can be used for the improvement of your own business.

Another feature of successful buying is to order seasonal goods well in advance of requirements when manufacturers are able to offer and guarantee delivery of their full range of products. If seasonal orders are placed too late, it may only be possible at that time to order lines which are of no interest to other retailers. A good example of this is in the toys, games, etc. trade, where manufacturers hold toy fairs to display their forthcoming Christmas range of products during February and March of each year. By placing an order early it does not necessarily mean that delivery of the goods must be accepted soon afterwards, as arrangements for delivery can be made to meet the convenience of the proprietor. As an example, again referring to a toy shop, it is possible to place an order in March for delivery during the following October or November, which is in good time for the Christmas trade.

Show interest in quantity discounts when offered, but at the same time bear in mind the selling potential of the product. For example, if it is intended to order 90 items of a particular line, and the representative draws attention to the fact that by increasing the order to 100 it will qualify for a quantity discount of $7\frac{1}{2}$ per cent, then the discount may be a proposition worthy of consideration. If, on the other hand, the quantity discount is not effective until a minimum order for 200 is given, an order to this extent may be in excess of the number which can be sold through the shop and is, therefore, of no value if an accumulation of unsaleable stock is to be avoided.

Perhaps the most difficult area, even for the experienced buyer, is in the field of fashion wear, which tends to be subject to violent and frequent change. Ladies' dresses, handbags and shoes are a good example of this where for every new fashion which succeeds, many are marketed and fail. One of the secrets of buying in trades dependent on changing fashion is to underorder if uncertainty exists regarding a new style, and then to repeat with perhaps a larger quantity if it becomes firmly established.

A chapter on buying would not be complete unless reference was made to the Voluntary Buying Group. To explain historically how the Voluntary Buying Group came into existence you must be reminded of the advantage that the large multiple chain has over the one man business. The multiple is able to order in large quantities and thus obtain a cheaper price for delivery direct to its shops by the manufacturer, or at an even keener price if all that is required of the manufacturer to fulfil the order is for him to deliver it in bulk to a central warehouse, and for its subsequent redistribution to retail outlets on transport owned by the multiple. To counter this competitive advantage several one man businesses combined together to form a Buying Group where, instead of each of them placing an order direct with a manufacturer or wholesaler, they totalled their individual requirements into one and obtained a lower price accordingly.

The trade in which the Voluntary Buying Group is most firmly established is in food distribution, where the system has proved to be the means of survival of many a one outlet grocer. Technically, Buying Groups in the grocery trade are becoming more sophisticated by reason of their success, and they are now able to offer incentives to attract new members in the form of finance on very favourable terms to encourage them to modernize their shop premises.

Voluntary Buying Groups are extending their horizons into other trades, such as do-it-yourself home maintenance, and it is suggested therefore that if one exists within your trade full details should be obtained of the scheme to enable you to judge whether any advantage will accrue by joining.

A more recent innovation in the distributive industry now establishing itself in many trades, again to attract the small man, is the 'Cash and Carry' depot which provides for a range of products to fully satisfy the requirements of a particular trade to be available at a central warehouse. This permits the small business proprietor to obtain all his supplies at cheaper prices, resulting from the warehouse buying in bulk, than would otherwise be possible if the proprietor purchased direct from a manufacturer or a traditional wholesaler.

7

CHAPTER 15

Advertising

The advantages of advertising to a manufacturer distributing his products on a national or regional scale are self-apparent; similarly are the advantages to a company retailing through a chain of outlets. In each case, due to the brand image or size of the companies, it is possible for them to beneficially bring their products or name before the public, who may then readily associate the advertisement with a product obtainable from or, a shop situated in, many of the High Streets throughout the country.

The position with regard to advertising is not so clear in the case of a proprietor of a one man business. He is isolated to the extent that his business is in a parade of shops, where it is possible for him to find that he is not selling a single product or offering any service which cannot be obtained from another shop in the same parade. This, therefore, largely restricts the opportunity of such a proprietor from making any real impact by advertising, and unless the objectives are well defined and the campaign thoroughly planned beforehand, any expenditure incurred may be of no avail.

If any benefit is to be received from an advertising campaign, a proprietor should consider the possibility of a constantly changing programme in terms of either special offers or services, the ideas of which need not themselves necessarily be new provided they are not being offered by any competitor at that moment of time or, alternatively, limiting the subject matter of the campaign to a simple one of promoting his business name, address and class of trade without reference to any other factor.

It has been established on many occasions that the greatest potential source of benefit from advertising for a small business is the general impression it radiates to the public who pass or enter the shop resulting from the observations already referred to in Chapter 13, such as special offers, the employment of polite assistants, the shop's general tidiness and the standard of the window display. The strength of the argument lies in the fact that, when circulated advertising matter is read, a housewife if attracted by its message has to make a special effort to visit the shop if she wishes to take immediate advantage of the offer or remember it for when she is next out shopping, with the possibility of the housewife failing to do either. The benefit to be derived by a business from its good impression is that the shopper is already outside the premises and in the mood for buying, and it only needs a little encouragement for her to enter and make a purchase without causing any additional inconvenience. As expenditure on shop fittings has already been incurred, it can also be claimed that this form of advertising, in addition to being the most satisfactory, is also free.

If it is decided to embark on an advertising campaign in the traditional sense, it is recommended first of all that an expenditure target is fixed, having regard to the amount which can be afforded, and the campaign planned accordingly by obtaining estimates in advance. Do not enter into advertising commitments ignoring beforehand the question of cost and adding the bills up later. Advertising expenditure can run away with itself unless closely controlled.

When promoting advertising for the purpose of continually bringing the name of the business to the attention of the public, a small display in a local paper, only referring to its name, address, class of trade and incorporating a short text, is all that is necessary. If the purpose of the advertisement is to announce a special offer or a new service which will be available for a limited period only, then a more extensive and forceful advertisement is justified.

Even in these days of a contracting newspaper industry, with local papers either merging or ceasing to publish, many areas are still served by two or more local newspapers and the problem arises of selecting the most suitable paper if the advertising budget allows for the use of only one of them. It is suggested that the advertisement should be inserted in the local newspaper with the largest circulation in the locality of the business, even though perhaps the paper concerned may have the lowest total circulation. The most popular paper may obtain its circulation by being strongly supported in a nearby town, and it must be accepted that not many customers will result from an advertisement involving them in a car or bus journey. A local newsagent will advise on the paper most strongly demanded in the area if this information is not already known.

Most local newspaper publishers offer reduced rates for period advertisements. Hence, if the advertisement is to be inserted for a number of consecutive weeks, order advertising space for the duration of the campaign to claim the rebate, as opposed to ordering the space on a week-to-week basis.

The spaces of a local newspaper usually considered to have the most impact for an advertisement are those available on the front and back pages and the right hand side of page three. As these pages are usually much in demand, a hint to help you obtain and then maintain your selected space, in addition to booking it well before hand, is to pay for the advertisements in advance of publication. Newspaper publishers are appreciative, in common with business generally, of customers who pay in this manner.

Local charity or church magazines are another outlet for advertising revenue. It is generally thought, however, that advertisements in magazines of this nature are limited in appeal, and an element of the advertising cost is usually considered to be a donation towards their respective funds. Another inexpensive medium which tends to show good returns is a screen advertisement displayed at the local cinema. A selection of standard films is available for each class of trade, leaving the advertiser to select the one which appeals to him most. The name and address of the advertiser and suitable dialogue are added to the screen play for him. The cost of the advertisement must obviously depend on the screen time of the advertisement, but an indication would be between £70 and £100 per quarter, in addition to a small initial charge, payable on the signing of the contract, which is sometimes demanded. Advertising space in buses, tubes and trains is another outlet, but in these cases it is sometimes considered that, for a small business to derive any benefit from such a campaign, it must be of a long term nature by continually displaying the name and address of the advertiser before the public. Bus stops are a different matter, as the location of the site can be determined by the advertiser in advance to meet his wishes. Bus commuters are finding this means of transport is taking up an ever increasing waiting time, and an advertisement in a bus shelter can prove to be of advantage, even allowing for the fact that they tend to be damaged and the subject matter and design of the advertisement must be frequently changed to hold interest.

Advertisement hoardings are also a possibility. Unfortunately a small business may find it extremely difficult to book an isolated hoarding, as the display companies find it more profitable and easier to sell their available space to companies advertising on a national scale.

Every proprietor appears to be inundated with representatives endeavouring to sell space on behalf of trade directories. A good case for advertising in a trade directory can be made out for a manufacturer who hopes to receive enquiries from buyers seeking alternative sources of supply where their only guide is invariably the trade classification section of a directory. So far as concerns a retail business, however, the author has never yet heard of a housewife referring to a trade directory before going out to shop and he would not recommend expenditure in this manner. Other than gratefully accepting all free insertions offered, the only directory worthy of consideration involving expenditure in the view of the author, is a semi-display advertisement in the Post Office 'Yellow Pages' Directory. It can be argued against this, of course, that the average member of the public must first remember the name of the business before looking in the Post Office Directory, thus defeating the whole object of the exercise, and in any event a free insertion will be available to every user of a business telephone, which will be adequate for the majority of businesses.

In all matters appertaining to advertising where, due to personal preferences, a campaign can be deemed a success or failure even before it starts, the author accepts that one person's opinion is probably as good as another's, but it is his experience that the method best suited to meet the needs of a one man business proprietor is the house-to-house distribution of cards or leaflets, especially if the campaign is to promote a special offer or a new service, as it can be localized to an area or areas as specified to obtain maximum benefit for every penny spent. Most firms of leaflet distributors offer a service to include the designing and the printing of the advertising matter.

The cost of an inclusive leaflet distribution campaign must, once again, depend on the printing costs, but it is usually reckoned to be between £4 and £8 per thousand leaflets distributed.

Certain aspects of advertising fall within the terms of the Trade Descriptions Act, 1964, to which reference is made in Chapter 19.

CHAPTER 16

Administration

Just as a permanently untidy shop area ought not to be tolerated, by the same token, neither should paperwork be dealt with in a haphazard fashion by its being allowed to fall seriously into arrear. Administration can be a nuisance, especially after a hard day's work, and it is very tempting at times to leave paperwork unattended to and hope that it will take care of itself which, of course, it never does. Make a habit of either reserving so much time each day, or certain days of each week, for dealing with the administrative matters which naturally arise from the conduct of any business.

With regard to bookkeeping, once a system has been selected ensure that it is maintained. The option is always open to file all invoices and other vouchers in a bag for the accountant to sort out once a year, but if this method is selected, then do not complain if he charges more than 40 guineas for his services.

It is possible to have a perfectly adequate system of bookkeeping, known as the single entry method, by only maintaining a cash book, a bought ledger and a sales ledger (the latter will only be necessary if sales on credit are to be permitted). With regard to writing up the bought and sales ledgers, take the duty seriously, as there is no point in working hard in the shop to make a profit and then throwing some of it needlessly away by not keeping the ledgers up to date, resulting in an overpayment to a supplier or perhaps even the omission of a sales invoice from the account of a customer. Furthermore, never pay a bought ledger account unless the balance has been reconciled with the supplier's statement, and again only if the documents are available to support each invoice, as already referred to in Chapter 14.

The main reason for supporting the necessity of reconciling a supplier's statement with his account in the bought ledger, is to safeguard against one of the most frequent causes of error, namely crediting a purchase invoice to an incorrect supplier's account. If payment is made from the bought ledger without first reconciling the account with a statement, then an overpayment of (say) £100 could be made to a supplier, only for you to receive in due course from the supplier who submitted the misposted invoice a reminder that £100 is still due to him, which will again have to be paid without guarantee that the supplier receiving the incorrect payment will refund the excess to you.

Regularly send out statements each month to customers with an account reflecting a balance in your favour, and do not hesitate to write requesting payment from those customers with an unpaid account which exceeds normal terms of credit.

One of the principal functions of a cash book is to provide information for ascertaining the up-to-date bank balance; therefore, all banking transactions should be regularly recorded therein.

Some proprietors cannot bother themselves with the mundane task of compiling a cash book and rely on an occasional telephone conversation with their bank manager for details of the balance as appearing on their account, and it is apathy of this nature which can cause serious difficulties. One such example is the drawing of a cheque for a large amount in favour of a supplier and the proprietor assuming that it has been debited to his account when a few days later he asks his bank for the current balance, whereas in fact the cheque has not been cleared. If the proprietor should then draw a further cheque based on this information, when both cheques are finally debited they may have the combined effect of exceeding the overdraft arrangement of the business and resulting in cheques being dishonoured, thus impairing future credit rating.

It is also essential at any given point of time to be able to assess the extent of the liabilities of a business. The maintenance of an up-to-date bought ledger will provide access to this information, as all that is necessary is for the balances in the ledger to be extracted in list form and then totalled. The total of the creditors can be compared with the balance available as per the cash book to ascertain if the business is becoming financially overcommitted. If early signs of financial instability are observed, then under no circumstances be tempted to add unnecessarily to your financial burden, even if it means letting a 'good thing' go, unless of course your bank manager is prepared to finance the specific project. Take comfort from the thought that there is always a better bargain round the corner, and when it does appear, the financial position may be healthier so that advantage can be taken of the opportunity without its endangering your business.

If a history could be written about every large company, with particular reference to how it grew from its humble origins, there would undoubtedly be a common factor to show that at some stage during each of their respective developments they were managed by an individual with a keen sense of using money to its full advantage.

Reference is made to double entry bookkeeping in the next chapter.

The thought of introducing a system of budgetary control into your business may be more than your blood pressure can reasonably withstand. In fact all that is necessary to install an effective system is to take a copy of the most recent financial accounts of the business, even if they relate to a year during which the business was under the ownership of the vendor, and to divide the turnover and items of expense by 12 to arrive at a monthly target for each item for the current period. The difference between the ascertained monthly turnover and total monthly expenses will represent the monthly budgeted profit. If this information is tabulated on analysis paper, then at the end of each month the actual turnover and expenses can be inserted against the budget and the two compared to assess the performance for the month and possible result of the year if trade continues at the same level. In the unlikely event of actual turnover and every item of expense equalling budget, this will indicate that the profit level of the previous year is being exactly maintained. If turnover is below budget and total expenditure is higher than budget, this will suggest that actual profit for the year may be less than that achieved during the previous year; conversely, if total expenses are less and turnover more than budget, the profit may be greater. As a method of controlling costs it is far better to ascertain early in the year that a particular item of expenditure is getting out of hand so that corrective action can be taken, than to be informed of the fact by your accountant at the year end, by which time it will be too late to redress. The procedure as described is an elementary budgetary control system, and yet if intelligently used will allow an opportunity of seeing an amber light before serious difficulties arise.

A more sophisticated system of budgetary control is first to calculate the number of shop opening days, allowing for holidays, including Bank Holidays, in each month throughout the financial year (12 accounting periods in the year), or in each period of exactly 4 weeks (13 accounting periods in the year). The advantage of a system involving 13 accounting periods is, of course, that each period will be more consistent with the other for the analysis of information as lies between calendar months. Whichever number of accounting periods is selected, the system should remain in operation for subsequent financial years to provide a basis for accurate comparison purposes when setting figures of any period against those of a corresponding period in a previous year.

When the number of accounting periods in each year has been established the next stage must be to budget the turnover for each period, having regard to the number of working days, historical information, seasonal fluctuations and the current trend in trade as indicated by a combination of your own turnover and national trading conditions. The difficulty of assessing future turnover is that, however thorough the information that is compiled, it may be seriously affected by circumstances beyond control as, for example, by the introduction of unforeseen Governmental fiscal measures.

Having budgeted the turnover, the estimated expenditure must then be apportioned between each accounting period. Many of the expenses may be allocated between the periods strictly on a *pro rata* time basis, e.g. rent, but certain expenses can be allocated to the periods in which the liabilities will actually be incurred, if known.

The budgeted net profit for each period will again be the difference between the monthly or 4 weekly estimated revenue and expenditure.

The actual turnover and expenditure for each financial period can be tabulated against its respective budgeted item to facilitate an assessment of the actual annual results if the trend for the current period applies for the remainder of the year.

A specimen layout of a budget is now shown to represent the business of the sole trader as reflected by the accounts in Chapter 5 in respect of the year following the period of the financial accounts, and also showing the position at the end of February after the insertion of the actual turnover and expenses for the 2 months:

The budgeted position for the year is that turnover is estimated to be £21,500 and gross profit £5,375 (25 per cent), leaving a resultant total net profit of £1,865. Of the total net profit it is anticipated that £104 will be earned in January, £94 in February, £17 in March, and so on, month by month. The gross profit for January is estimated to be only 21 per cent against the average for the year of 25 per cent, due to anticipated price reductions during a sales period to be held in that month. Concerning budgeted expenditures, they have

A Sole Trad

Revenue and Expenditure for

	January		February		Two Months Total	
	Budget	Actual	Budget	Actual	Budget	Actua
Turnover	1,730	1,710	1,670	1,760	3,400	3,470
Less : Cost of goods sold, i.e. Purchases after adjusting for opening and closing stocks	1,365	1,368	1,270	1,302	2,635	2,670
Gross profit	365	342	400	458	765	800
Gross profit (%)	21·0	20·0	24·0	26·0	23·0	23·0
Wages	85	77	90	104	175	181
Rent	45	45	45	45	90	90
General and water rates	25	23	25	23	50	46
Insurances	4	5	3	3	7	8
Lighting and heating	25	22	20	20	45	42
Telephone	3	3	3	3	6	6
Packing materials	15	17	20	19	35	36
Printing and stationery	2	2	2	2	4	4
Postages	1	1	1	2	2	3
Motor expenses	20	16	20	17	40	33
Repairs to premises	—	—	20	17	20	17
Advertising	—	—	—	40	—	40
Bank interest and charges	1	1	1	1	2	2
Accountancy charges	4	4	4	4	8	8
Sundry expenses	10	9	30	24	40	33
Depreciation :						
Fixtures and fittings	4	4	5	5	9	9
Motor car	17	17	17	17	34	34
	261	246	306	346	567	592
Net profit	104	96	94	112	198	208

Note :

When apportioning the annual budgeted turnover and expenditure into monthly or 4 wee budgets, absolute accuracy is not necessary. If large enough, the sums may be rounc off to the nearest £5 and to the nearest £1 in other cases.

get

r Ending 31st December 19..

March		Three Months Total			Total for Year	
dget	Actual	Budget	Actual		Budget	Actual
840		5,240			21,500	
360		3,995			16,125	
480		1,245			5,375	
6·0		24·0			25·0	
90		265		Continue for	1,100	
50		140		←— Months of April —→	550	
25		75		to December	300	
3		10			40	
15		60			180	
2		8			35	
15		50			200	
3		7			30	
1		3			10	
25		65			250	
170		190			300	
30		30			60	
1		3			10	
5		13			50	
5		45			130	
5		14			55	
18		52			210	
463		1,030			3,510	
17		215			1,865	

generally been opportioned on a time basis, rounded off to the nearest £5 in many instances, but there are items which have been analysed to comply with estimated use, light and heat, or when the expenditure will be incurred, i.e. repairs to premises, £170, and advertising, £30, both during March.

With regard to the actual results, a proprietor could consider at the end of February that as his actual profit is £208, being £10 in excess of the budgeted profit of £198, he need take no further action as his level of profit is better than the one he anticipated. On the other hand, a proprietor could recognize the foregoing and ask himself how he could do even better. Two observations which are apparent from the information are, first, why was the expenditure for wages during February (£104) in excess of budget (£90) and, second, for what reason was advertising expenditure of £40 incurred during February when none was contemplated? An investigation may reveal that an additional shop assistant is being unnecessarily employed so far as the wage expenditure is concerned and that the advertising campaign was brought forward as a last minute decision from March to February. With regard to the former, by reducing the number of assistants the profit position could be improved even more.

A personal factor which helps to make a success of a business is an attitude of mind which readily recognizes mistakes, especially those made by oneself. Mistakes will be made, but worrying about them afterwards will not relieve the position and in any event while doing so, other mistakes may be made.

One area in which errors frequently occur is in the field of buying. Many proprietors order products which are subsequently found to be slow moving, or even unsaleable, and instead of getting out of their predicament as best as they are able they become stubborn and insist on selling the products only at full price. This type of proprietor will over a period of time tie up many hundreds of pounds in obsolete stock, the equivalent of dead money.

Finally, never consider the absolute secret of success has been found, as success is only relative to current standards which are continually changing, usually for the better. Be open minded to new techniques and ideas and be willing to listen to anyone who is prepared to offer advice. Unnecessary expense can be incurred on trade magazines, but no harm is done by subscribing to one or two of the better journals servicing your trade to keep abreast of current events.

CHAPTER 17

Double Entry Bookkeeping

Any method of bookkeeping which fully satisfies the needs of a proprietor to yield the basic information he considers necessary must be regarded as adequate. But as in the case of the equality of man where some men are more equal than others, some methods of bookkeeping are more adequate than others.

The system of bookkeeping which is generally recognized as being the most satisfactory from the aspect of reducing to a minimum the possibility of losses through errors, and from the view of enabling essential information to be extracted from the books of account in the quickest possible time, is the one known as the 'double entry method'.

If two columns are drawn and inserted in each, any or as many numbers as you care to enter (provided every number written in the left hand column is also entered in the right hand column and the two columns are totalled) they must obviously equal one another. This is the basic principle of 'double entry' bookkeeping where, for every debit entry (left hand column) there must be a corresponding credit entry (right hand column), so that at the end of any given financial period if the net balances reflected in every ledger account are listed the debit side must equal the credit side. With this agreement, it can safely be assumed that the transactions recorded during the period are arithmetically correct. The list of balances referred to is known as the 'trial balance'.

It should be clear that a business cannot conduct the recording of all its financial transactions by the use of one ledger only, as the volume and variety of entries would make the ledger too large and hence too unwieldy to handle. Therefore, a number of books must be provided. The books of account necessary to furnish a small business with a satisfactory double entry bookkeeping system can be restricted to:

1 Ledgers of prime entry, i.e. books directly concerned with the double entry system:

a Cash book.
b Petty cash book.
c Bought ledger.
d Sales ledger (only if sales on credit are to be permitted).
e Nominal ledger, and

2 Subsidiary books which, although they in themselves do not form part of the double entry, their employment is essential as a matter of convenience to restrict to a minimum the volume of transactions which would otherwise appear in the books of prime entry:
f Sales day book (only if sales on credit are to be permitted).
g Bought day book.

The function of the accounting books mentioned against items (*a*) to (*d*) has already been referred to. The nominal ledger may be regarded as the pivot of the system, as it is the ledger into which all transactions in the other ledgers and books are finally recorded under relevant accounting classifications for the purposes of enabling the trial balance to be extracted and the financial accounts prepared. The sales day book, which represents neither the debit nor credit side, is effectively a summary of the sales on credit compiled from copy invoices issued to credit customers and acts as a posting medium. The day book is used to record the individual entries to the debit of the customers' accounts in the sales ledger and the total sales for the period to the credit of the sales account in the nominal ledger. The bought day book serves a similar purpose as the sales day book, again representing neither debit nor credit, except that it is used to summarize purchase invoices. The entries in the bought day book are debited to the relevant expense accounts in the nominal ledger and the individual transactions to the credit of the various suppliers' accounts in the bought ledger.

The factor which appears to cause most concern in the understanding of double entry bookkeeping is the distinction between debit and credit and the account which should show the former entry and the account to reflect the credit. Once this principle has been grasped, the other principles appear to fall into place more readily. The author has read many definitions of the meaning of debit and credit, but they never assisted him to any extent during the period when he was an articled clerk, struggling to understand the basic principles involved, so it is therefore proposed to tackle the problem from another angle.

The book of account which is perhaps most generally understood is the cash book, and it will therefore be used to form the basis of conveying the meaning of debit and credit entries where cash and cheque transactions are concerned. Receipts of cash or cheques are debit entries in the cash book, and the payment of cash or cheques are credits. An example of transactions as affecting a cash book (ignoring any question of purchases and sales on credit) is as follows:

A Sole Trader commences business on the 1st July as a tobacconist starting with a capital of £1,000.

On the 1st July he buys cigarettes and other smokers' requisites amounting to £600, drawing a cheque in settlement, and achieves sales of £40.

On 2nd July he pays rent for the quarter in advance of £150 and makes sales of £45.

Sales for 3rd July are £47.

Sales for 4th July are £53.

Sales for 5th July are £49.

On 6th July sales of £58 are attained, and smokers' requisites purchased at a cost of £140.

Prepare cash book for the week.

Once the entry in the cash book has been established it must necessarily follow that the corresponding posting to complete the double entry must be a credit in the case of a receipt (debit in the cash book), and a debit in respect of a payment (credit in the cash book).

If all transactions were immediately settled by cheque or cash no problems as to debit or credit would arise. Unfortunately, with regard to purchases and sales on credit, by their very nature entries must first be made to ensure that they are not forgotten before the question of settlement by cheque or cash arises and another memory aid is necessary. It is suggested for the initial entries of credit transactions that the sales and purchases accounts in the nominal ledger be used where a credit sale is posted to the credit of the sales account and a credit purchase is debited to one of the expenses accounts in the nominal ledger. Having established this fact, the debit of a sale on credit is an entry in a customer's account in the sales ledger and

A Sole Trader

Cash Book

DR   **CR**

Receipts							Payments					
19..		Folio	Total	Sales	Ledger		19..		Folio	Total	Purchases	Ledger
July 1	To Capital a/c		1,000 0 0		Capital a/c 1,000 0 0		July 1	By Purchases		600 0 0	600 0 0	
2	Sales		40 0 0	40 0 0			2	Rent		150 0 0		Rent a/c 150 0 0
3	Sales		45 0 0	45 0 0			6	Purchases		140 0 0	140 0 0	
4	Sales		47 0 0	47 0 0								
5	Sales		53 0 0	53 0 0							740 0 0	150 0 0
6	Sales		49 0 0	49 0 0			6	Balance	C/D	890 0 0		
	Sales		58 0 0	58 0 0						402 0 0		
			1,292 0 0	292 0 0	1,000 0 0					1,292 0 0		
July 7	To Balance	B/D	402 0 0									

the credit posting in respect of a purchase is to a supplier's account in the bought ledger.

To reiterate the paragraphs concerning debit and credit entries the position may be summarized as follows.

If cash or cheques are directly involved, then consider the transactions in the cash book and:

1 If a receipt, the entry must be a debit in the cash book with the corresponding second entry a credit.

2 If a payment, the entry must be a credit in the cash book with the corresponding second entry a debit.

If the cash book is not directly affected, i.e. a credit transaction, then think of the sales or expense accounts in the nominal ledger and:

3 If a sale is on credit, the sales account in the nominal ledger must be credited and the customer's account in the sales ledger debited.

4 If the transaction is a purchase on credit, an expense account in the nominal ledger must be debited and supplier's account in the bought ledger credited.

When cash or cheques are subsequently received or paid in respect of credit transactions they will fall within the procedures referred to against (1) and (2) above.

The distinction must now be drawn between capital and revenue expenditure. Capital expenditure relates to the purchase of assets, the benefits of which will be available to the business for a given period of time. Revenue expenditure is the cost of the goods sold and all the ancillary expenditure involved in selling them, including for this purpose the cost of repairs to and depreciation of fixed assets. The treatment of the two classes of expenditure is entirely different. Capital expenditure is debited to an asset account in the nominal ledger and shown on the balance sheet as such, whereas revenue expenditure is eventually debited to the trading account or profit and loss account for the financial period and written off as a charge against income accordingly.

Referring again to the trial balance, it must follow that if the two sides fail to reconcile, somewhere within the mass of transactions recorded for a period at least one mistake must have occurred, and before any further use can be made of the trial balance a programme of checking must be undertaken to find the difference. Such a

8

programme should be working from one routine to the next until the error is found as follows:

1 Go through each account in the nominal ledger to check all additions and confirm that the balances have been extracted onto the trial balance correctly.

2 Re-add all additions and any cross casts in the books of prime entry, sales day book and bought day book.

3 Check all postings from the cash book, petty cash book and sales and bought day books, particularly noting that double entry principles have applied in all cases. A debit in one book of £20 posted to the debit of another account will have the effect of doubling itself as a difference, i.e. the trial balance will reflect the debit side as being £40 in excess of the credits.

4 Ensure that every debit entry has a corresponding credit entry. If only one entry is made in the books it is referred to as a 'blind' entry.

5 Check for accuracy the original extraction of balances from the sales and bought ledgers.

Unfortunately there are five types of errors which a trial balance will not disclose even if it is arithmetically correct. They are:

1 Errors of commission.
2 Errors of omission.
3 Errors of original entry.
4 Errors of principle.
5 Compensating errors.

1 Errors of commission apply when postings are made to the incorrect account of the same class. A cheque drawn in favour of a supplier, S. T. Brown & Co., is posted to the debit of G. E. Brown Ltd. The double entry principle has not been violated and therefore the error will not reflect itself in the trial balance. All that has happened is the balance due to S. T. Brown & Co. will show a credit of £100 in excess of the true position, and the amount in favour of G. E. Brown Ltd. will reflect a balance of £100 less than the correct one.

2 Errors of omission are, as the name implies, where an entry which should appear in the books is omitted altogether. An invoice from W. Wilson Co. Ltd. for £150 for purchases is lost immediately on

receipt; therefore both the debit side (purchases account) and credit side of the account of W. Wilson & Co. Ltd. will be deficient of £150.

3 Errors of original entry may be explained by again referring to a purchase invoice from W. Wilson & Co. Ltd. for £125 10s 0d which is entered in the bought day book as £125. Because the day book is used as the posting medium for writing up the nominal ledger and bought ledger the subsequent two entries will also be deficient to the extent of 10s 0d.

4 Errors of principle are entries into the wrong class of account, such as the buying of shop fittings for own use and posted to the debit of a revenue account instead of to the debit of an asset account.

5 Compensating errors are incorrect entries or additions on the debit side compensated by unrelated but equalizing errors on the credit side as, for example, a debit entry omitted to be posted of £50 being offset by an underaddition of £50 in the sales account in the nominal ledger.

Examples will now be given of the use of the books of account as mentioned earlier, with the exception of the cash book (already shown) and nominal ledger (a specimen of which will be submitted later).

Petty Cash Book

A sole trader maintains a petty cash book with an opening balance of cash-in-hand of £7 and incurs the following petty cash transactions:

			£
1st	July	Paid for printing	4
2nd	July	Paid for postage stamps	2
3rd	July	Cashed cheque to supplement petty cash balance	50
4th	July	Paid for tea	1
		Paid for stationery	3
		Paid for telegram	1
		Paid for fares	1
5th	July	Paid for stamps	2
		Paid for printing	6
		Paid for carriage	4
		Paid for sugar	2

A Sole Trader
Petty Cash Book

Receipts	Folio No.	Date	Particulars	Voucher No.	Total	Printing and stationery	Postage and cables	Carriage	Sundry expenses	Nominal ledger
7 0 0		July 1	Balance B/D							
			Printing	1	4 0 0	4 0 0				
		2	Postages	2	2 0 0		2 0 0			
50 0 0		3	Cheque							
		4	Tea	3	1 0 0				1 0 0	
			Stationery	4	3 0 0	3 0 0				
			Telegram	5	1 0 0		1 0 0			
			Fares	6	1 0 0				1 0 0	
		5	Stamps	7	2 0 0		2 0 0			
			Printing	8	6 0 0	6 0 0				
			Carriage	9	4 0 0			4 0 0		
			Sugar	10	2 0 0				2 0 0	
			Stamps	11	2 0 0		2 0 0			
		6	Printing	12	6 0 0	6 0 0				
			Light fittings	13	20 0 0					Asset a/c 20 0 0
					54 0 0	19 0 0	7 0 0	4 0 0	4 0 0	20 0 0
57 0 0		6	Balance	C/D	3 0 0					
3 0 0		July 7	Balance	B/D	57 0 0					

6th July	Paid for stamps	2
	Paid for printing	6
	Paid for light fittings	20

Show the entries as they should appear in the petty cash book.

The completion of the double entry in respect of the items recorded in the petty cash book will be a credit to the cash book to counterbalance the cheque drawn of £50 (so far as the cash book is concerned the cheque must be considered a payment), and with regard to the items of expense in the petty cash book, the corresponding entries will be the debiting of the totals in the analysis columns to their respective accounts in the nominal ledger. The total expenditure column in this case will not be used for posting purposes as its function is to act as an arithmetical control for the cross cast of the analysis columns and to calculate the cash-in-hand as at the close of business on the 6th July.

The petty cash book as prepared indicates that whenever the cash balance runs low a further sum of money is paid into the account to finance further petty cash expenditure. This practice of drawing irregular amounts as required may cause concern to a proprietor over a period of time if he should engage clerical assistance as he will never be sure of the extent of the petty cash float and also he will not be able to control the amount of expenditure, both of which may result in monetary losses. A refinement of this haphazard procedure is known as the imprest system, involving the fixing of the petty cash float at a convenient figure to adequately cover the normal petty cash expenses of a regular period, say 7 days, at the end of which the petty cash book is ruled off and a cheque cashed to equal the actual expenditure incurred during the chosen period. Therefore if the float is fixed at £50, at any given time the petty cash account must be able to produce £50 either in cash or petty cash vouchers, thus achieving a limited degree of control.

Bought Ledger and Bought Day Book

A sole trader incurs the following liabilities:

1st July	Received invoice from	J. Gregg & Co.	for £130	Purchase of goods for resale

	Received invoice from	T. Wilson & Co.	for £35	Purchase of goods for resale
2nd July	Received invoice from	S. Walker Ltd.	for £170	Purchase of goods for resale
	Received invoice from	National Electric Co. Ltd.	for £15	Electricity
	Received invoice from	B. Smith Ltd.	for £60	Purchase of goods for resale
3rd July	Received invoice from	J. Gregg & Co.	for £70	Purchase of goods for resale
	Drew cheque in favour of	J. Gregg & Co.	for £130	
4th July	Received invoice from	Hornly District Council	for £75	Rates
	Received invoice from	Telephone Co. Ltd.	for £11	Telephone account
	Received invoice from	B. Allen	for £17	Repairs to machinery
5th July	Received invoice from	J. Gregg & Co.	for £68	Purchase of goods for resale
	Received invoice from	T. Wilson & Co.	for £178	Purchase of goods for resale
6th July	Received invoice from	J. Gregg & Co.	for £112	Purchase of goods for resale
	Drew cheque in favour of	J. Gregg & Co.	for £250	
	Drew cheque in favour of	T. Wilson & Co.	for £213	
	Drew cheque in favour of	S. Walker Ltd.	for £100	On account
	Drew cheque in favour of	National Electric Co. Ltd.	for £15	

Show the entries as they should appear in the bought day book and bought ledger.

The entries necessary in respect of the foregoing example to complete the double entry are:

1 With regard to cheques drawn in favour of the suppliers by a credit to the cash book, and

2 In respect of the invoices, by debiting the total of each analysis column of the day book to its respective account in the nominal ledger.

A Sole Trader

Bought Day Book

Page 1

Date	Supplier	Folio No.	Total	Purchases	Repairs to machinery	Tele-phone	Elec-tricity	Nominal ledger	
July 1	J. Gregg & Co.	2	130 0 0	130 0 0					
	T. Wilson & Co.	8	35 0 0	35 0 0					
2	S. Walker Ltd.	7	170 0 0	170 0 0					
	National Electric Co. Ltd.	4	15 0 0				15 0 0		
	B. Smith Ltd.	5	60 0 0	60 0 0					
3	J. Gregg & Co.	2	70 0 0	70 0 0					
4	Hornly District Council	3	75 0 0					Rates	75 0 0
	Telephone Co. Ltd.	6	11 0 0			11 0 0			
	B. Allen	1	17 0 0		17 0 0				
5	J. Gregg & Co.	2	68 0 0	68 0 0					
	T. Wilson & Co.	8	178 0 0	178 0 0					
6	J. Gregg & Co.	2	112 0 0	112 0 0					
			941 0 0	823 0 0	17 0 0	11 0 0	15 0 0		75 0 0

Bought Ledger

1

B. Allen

DR   CR

		Folio No.		19..		Folio No.	
				July 4	By Goods	1	17 0 0

2

J. Gregg and Co.

19..				19..			
July 3	To Cheque	CB	130 0 0	July 1	By Goods	1	130 0 0
6	Cheque	CB	250 0 0	3	Goods	1	70 0 0
				5	Goods	1	68 0 0
				6	Goods	1	112 0 0
			380 0 0				380 0 0

3

Hornly District Council

				19..			
				July 4	By Goods	1	75 0 0

DR   CR

4   National Electric Co. Ltd.

19..				19..			
July 6	To Cheque	CB	15 0 0	July 2	By Goods	1	15 0 0

5   B. Smith Ltd.

				19..			
				July 2	By Goods	1	60 0 0

6   Telephone Co. Ltd.

				19..			
				July 4	By Goods	1	11 0 0

7   S. Walker Ltd.

19..				19..			
July 6	To Cheque	CB	100 0 0	July 2	By Goods	1	170 0 0
	Balance	C/D	70 0 0				
			170 0 0				170 0 0
				19..			
				July 6	By Balance	B/D	70 0 0

8   T. Wilson and Co.

19..				19..			
July 6	To Cheque	CB	213 0 0	July 1	By Goods	1	35 0 0
				5	Goods	1	178 0 0
			213 0 0				213 0 0

It is appropriate at this stage to introduce the control account. For the purposes of this textbook a control account will relate only to the accounting entries as affecting credit sales and credit purchases and may be regarded as a trial balance within a trial balance. Assume for the moment that when the master trial balance is prepared it reflects a difference, then it may be necessary to check every entry recorded during the period in an attempt to find it, which can be both a long and tedious job. If a sales ledger control account and purchase ledger control account are both in operation within a bookkeeping system and the trial balance is out of balance, while at the same time it can be shown that the two control accounts agree, then the procedure for checking entries to trace the difference can be considerably reduced by limiting it to those transactions outside the credit sales and credit purchases day books and ledgers. To take a further example, if the totals of the trial balance show that the debit side is in excess of the credit column by £150, and this amount is the exact difference on the sales ledger control account, all that is necessary to find the difference is to restrict the cross checking to the sales ledger and its ancillary books as it must be contained within this area, and when found it will have the effect of agreeing the trial balance also.

The control account for the bought ledger and bought day book of the example as shown should be compiled as follows.

A Sole Trader
DR				Bought Ledger Control Account			CR
19.. July 6	To Cheques: Gregg Gregg Wilson Walker National Electric	CB CB CB CB CB	130 0 0 250 0 0 213 0 0 100 0 0 15 0 0	19.. July 6	By Goods	PDB 1	941 0 0
	Balances: Allen 17 0 0 Hornly 75 0 0 Smith 60 0 0 T'phone 11 0 0 Walker 70 0 0	C/D 1 3 5 6 7	708 0 0 233 0 0				
			941 0 0				941 0 0
				19.. July 6	By Balances	B/D	233 0 0

In practice the cheques drawn in favour of the suppliers would not be entered in the control account individually but posted in total as £708 from the cash book, which is not shown in this solution.

One further matter to be mentioned concerns the purchase of goods from a supplier which are subsequently returned to him for some reason, such as the goods being of a faulty design. The standard accountancy textbook will suggest all purchase credit notes should be separately recorded in a purchase returns day book, but in fact, all that is necessary to deal with them is to enter the credit notes in red in the purchase day book and to subtract the credit notes when totalling the columns in the day book. The entries for a purchase credit note are a debit to the supplier's account in the bought ledger and a credit to the purchases account in the nominal ledger, which will be achieved if recorded in the day book in red, as the total to be credited to the purchase account will be reduced to the extent of the said credit note. This procedure will avoid the necessity of introducing further day books into the bookkeeping system.

Sales Ledger and Sales Day Book

The basic principles of bookkeeping for recording transactions in the sales ledger and sales day book are basically the same as explained in the previous example, with the exception of the entries being reversed, i.e. debits in the expense account become credits in the sales account in the nominal ledger, and credits appearing in the bought ledger become debits in the sales ledger.

A sole trader invoices the following sales on credit terms.

1st July	J. Hilton & Co.	£140
	T. Brown Ltd.	£110
	B. Green & Co.	£230
2nd July	B. Green & Co.	£17
	P. Lowton Ltd.	£290
	J. Hilton & Co.	£30
3rd July	T. Brown Ltd.	£55
	T. Brown Ltd.	£70
4th July	Cheque received from T. Brown Ltd. for	£100 On account
5th July	R. Smith	£240
	P. Lowton Ltd.	£75
6th July	T. Brown Ltd.	£90
	Cheques received from : J. Hilton & Co.	for £170
	T. Brown Ltd.	for £200
	B. Green & Co.	for £247
	P. Lowton Ltd.	for £365

A Sole Trader
Sales Day Book

Page 1

Date	Customer	Folio No.	Total		
July 1	J. Hilton & Co.	3	140	0	0
	T. Brown Ltd.	1	110	0	0
	B. Green & Co.	2	230	0	0
2	B. Green & Co.	2	17	0	0
	P. Lowton Ltd.	4	290	0	0
	J. Hilton & Co.	3	30	0	0
3	T. Brown Ltd.	1	55	0	0
	T. Brown Ltd.	1	70	0	0
5	R. Smith	5	240	0	0
	P. Lowton Ltd.	4	75	0	0
6	T. Brown Ltd.	1	90	0	0
			1,347	0	0

It should be noted at this stage that it is not so essential to analyse sales in the sales day book as shown in the example of the purchase day book, as all types of sales are usually treated as one class; hence a total column is all that is required. Some proprietors, however, find it useful to ascertain the total sales of certain products and use the analysis columns for the purpose of calculating this information.

Sales Ledger

DR   CR

1   T. Brown Ltd.

19..		Folio No.		19..		Folio No.	
July 1	To Goods	1	110 0 0	July 4	By Cheque	CB	100 0 0
3	Goods	1	55 0 0	6	Cheque	CB	200 0 0
	Goods	1	70 0 0		Balance	C/D	25 0 0
6	Goods	1	90 0 0				
			325 0 0				325 0 0
19..							
July 6	To Balance	B/D	25 0 0				

2   B. Green & Co.

19..				19..			
July 1	To Goods	1	230 0 0	July 6	By Cheque	CB	247 0 0
2	Goods	1	17 0 0				
			247 0 0				247 0 0

3   J. Hilton & Co.

19..				19..			
July 1	To Goods	1	140 0 0	July 6	By Cheque	CB	170 0 0
2	Goods	1	30 0 0				
			170 0 0				170 0 0

4   P. Lowton Ltd.

19..				19..			
July 2	To Goods	1	290 0 0	July 6	By Cheque	CB	365 0 0
5	Goods	1	75 0 0				
			365 0 0				365 0 0

DR 5				R. Smith			CR
19..		Folio No.				Folio No.	
July 5	To Goods	1	240 0 0				

To complete the double entry of the transactions in this exercise the sales account in the nominal ledger will be credited with £1,347 and the cash book will show the cheques received from debtors as debits.

To finalize this example the sale ledger control account is shown.

A Sole Trader
DR   Sales Ledger Control Account   CR

19.. July 6	To Goods	SDB 1	1,347 0 0	19.. July 6	By Cheques:		
					Brown	CB	100 0 0
					Hilton	CB	170 0 0
					Brown	CB	200 0 0
					Green	CB	247 0 0
					Lowton	CB	365 0 0
							1,082 0 0
					Balances	C/D	
					Brown 25 0 0	1	
					Smith 240 0 0	5	265 0 0
			1,347 0 0				1,347 0 0
19.. July 6	To Balances	B/D	265 0 0				

Cash Discounts

Many businesses offer a cash discount as an inducement to debtors for them to pay their outstanding accounts promptly. A frequent example is a cash discount of $2\frac{1}{2}$ per cent off the amount due if a remittance is received by the creditor before the end of the month in which the invoice was raised.

Unlike a trade discount which is dealt with as a deduction from a purchase on the invoice a cash discount is considered to be a reward for the prompt use of money and, as such, discounts received and discounts allowed appear in the profit and loss account.

From the bookkeeping position cash discounts are analysed in 'memorandum' columns contained in the cash book, as they do not as this stage form part of the double entry system.

An extract from a cash book showing discount columns is shown below.

A Sole Trader
Cash Book (analysis columns ignored)

Receipts				Payments					CR
	Folio No.	Discounts allowed	Bank	19..		Folio No.	Discounts received	Bank	
		(Memo.)					(Memo.)		
To S. Smith		2 10 0	97 10 0	July 1	By T. Weller		8 10 0	161 10 0	
B. Brown Ltd.		1 10 0	58 10 0		F. Folley		1 15 0	68 5 0	
		4 0 0					10 5 0		

From the above information it can be assumed that the sole trader is offering a cash discount of 2½ per cent, F. Folley a discount of 2½ per cent and T. Weller a discount of 5 per cent.

The double entry for the discount allowed column is a debit of £4 to the discounts allowed account in the nominal ledger and credit entries of £2 10s 0d and £1 10s 0d to the respective debtors' accounts. With regard to discounts received, the supplier's accounts are debited with £8 10s 0d and £1 15s 0d, respectively, and the discounts receivable account in the nominal ledger credited with £10 5s 0d.

Bank Reconciliations

A regular monthly duty of any proprietor must be to confirm the accuracy of his cash book with that of the bank statement. This arises from the possibility of incorrect entries appearing in or omitted from the cash book, perhaps originating from interruptions caused by day-to-day pressures of conducting a business and forms one of the important functions of bookkeeping, namely to ensure there is always available the means of ascertaining the actual financial position of a business.

When the balance as shown in the cash book is compared with the one in the bank statement it is often found that the two balances are at variance with one another because:

1 When a cheque is drawn in favour of a creditor and entered in the cash book 3 days or more may elapse before it appears on the bank statement of the drawer. The period of 3 days is the time taken for a cheque to pass from the payee's bank account to the account of the drawer via the Bank Clearing House.

2 When a receipt is paid into a bank other than at the branch maintaining the account of the payee the same period of at least 3 days will again elapse before the bank account of the payee is credited. Receipts paid into a branch holding the account of the payee are normally credited on the statement during the same day.

There is a standard procedure for reconciling a cash book with a bank statement, as shown by the following example.

A Sole Trader
Cash Book (analysis columns ignored)

DR	Receipts				Payments				CR
19..		Folio No.	Bank	19..		Cheque No.	Folio No.		Bank
July 1	To Balance	B/D	1,235 0 0 ✓	July 1	By Wages	122			132 0 0 ✓
	Debtor		170 0 0 ✓		Rent	3			375 0 0 ✓
2	Debtor		230 0 0 ✓		Creditor	4			640 0 0 ✓
	Debtor		375 0 0 ✓		Creditor	5			77 0 0 ✓
3	Debtor		74 0 0 ✓		Creditor	6			39 0 0 ✓
4	Debtor		68 0 0 ✓	3	Insurance	7			54 0 0 ✓
	Debtor		39 0 0 ✓		Creditor	8			137 0 0 ✓
5	Debtor		78 0 0 ✓	3	Creditor	9			23 0 0 ✓
	Debtor		34 0 0 ✓		Creditor	130			16 0 0 ✓
	Debtor		130 0 0 ✓	5	Creditor	1			569 0 0
	Debtor		142 0 0 ✓		Subscription	2			20 0 0
6	Debtor		192 0 0		Creditor	3			104 0 0
	Debtor		14 0 0 ✓	6	Creditor	4			17 0 0
			2,781 0 0						2,203 0 0
					Balance		C/D		578 0 0
			2,781 0 0						2,781 0 0
19..				19..					
July 7	To Balance	B/D	578 0 0	July 7	Bank charges				25 0 0

It is assumed that the bank pass book as at 6th July will read as detailed after noting that receipts in a cash book are recorded on the bank statement as a credit entry and payments in a cash book as debits.

A Sole Trader
In account with Newtown Bank Ltd.

Account No. 1673122

For customer's use	Detail	Debits	Credits	Date	Balance
			Balance forward		1,235 0 0 √
	CT		170 0 0 √	July 1	
	122	132 0 0 √			1,273 0 0
	CT		230 0 0 √	2	
	CT		375 0 0 √		1,878 0 0
	CT		74 0 0 √	3	1,952 0 0
	126	39 0 0 √		4	
	124	640 0 0 √			
	123	375 0 0 √			
	125	77 0 0 √			
	CT		68 0 0 √		
	CT		39 0 0 √		928 0 0
	CT		78 0 0 √	5	
	CT		34 0 0 √		
	CT		130 0 0 √		
	CT		142 0 0 √		1,312 0 0
	129	23 0 0 √		6	
	127	54 0 0 √			
	128	137 0 0 √			
	130	16 0 0 √			
	CT		14 0 0 √		
	Charges	25 0 0			1,071 0 0

The amounts which are ticked appear in both the cash book and bank statement; hence the balance in the cash book of £578 must differ from the balance of £1,071 shown on the bank statement by reason of the five uncleared items in the cash book (one receipt and four payments) and one uncleared item in the bank statement. With regard to the latter, it is the practice of banks to debit accounts with their charges and interest without previously communicating this information to customers, and therefore it is not possible for a proprietor to write bank charges into his cash book until ascertaining the cost from the statement.

The reconciliation should take the form of working from the balance as per the bank statement to that of the cash book.

A Sole Trader
Bank Reconciliation as at 6th July 19..

Balance as per bank statement				1,071	0	0
Add : Receipts in cash book but not cleared				192	0	0
				1,263	0	0
Less : Payments in cash book but not cleared						
	131	569	0 0			
	2	20	0 0			
	3	104	0 0			
	4	17	0 0	710	0	0
				553	0	0
Add : Payment not in cash book				25	0	0
Balance as per cash book				£578	0	0

To summarize generally:

1 Tick on the bank statement and cash book all items which appear in both.

2 Calculate from the balance as shown on the statement to reconcile with the cash book balance.

If the final balance on the statement is in credit:

3 Add to it all receipts in the cash book which do not appear in the statement, and

4 Deduct receipts shown on the statement but which do not appear in the cash book.

5 Deduct from the balance as per bank statement all payments in the cash book which do not appear in the statement, and

6 Add all payments appearing in the statement but not shown in the cash book.

If the final balance on the statement reflects an overdraft position, the identical procedure to the above still applies, except for 'deduct' read 'add', and for 'add' read 'deduct' where referred to in (3) to (6) (inclusive) of the summary.

A worked example will now be shown to cover at least one entry of every type which a proprietor is likely to meet during the normal course of bookkeeping. The folio references used are in sequence to assist the reader and not necessarily those as will be used in practice, where it is found that folio numbers sometimes overlap to cause complications if the originating entry has to be referred to.

A sole trader commences business as a grocer on 1st July 19— and incurs the following transactions:

1st July	Paid into the business bank account the sum of £5,000 as capital.
	Paid £600 by cheque for the lease of the business premises with 10 years unexpired.
	Purchased shop fittings for own use amounting to £1,600 (depreciation to be charged at $7\frac{1}{2}$ per cent per annum, straight line method) drawing a cheque in settlement on the same day.
	Purchased stock for resale by cheque of £1,750.
	Purchased stock on credit of £1,600 for resale from Grocery Warehouse Ltd.
	Purchased stock on credit for resale of £670 from Northern Distributors Ltd.
	Paid rent of £300 for the quarter to 30th September.
	Cashed cheque for £50 for petty cash.
	Cash sales £94 (banked).
	Paid through petty cash £40 for packaging material.
2nd July	Cash sales £102 (banked).
	Credit sale £48 Welcome Caterers Ltd.
3rd July	Cash sales £109 (banked £89 and £20 retained for petty cash).
	Purchased goods for resale on credit from Grocery Warehouse Ltd. £470.
	Paid rates by cheque of £210 for quarter to 30th September.
4th– 10th July	Cash Sales £730 (banked).
7th July	Paid wages £28 (net).
	Paid self from petty cash £15 drawings.
11th July	Credit sale £37 Welcome Caterers Ltd.
	Drew cheques in favour of :
	Grocery Warehouse Ltd. for £1,000 on account.
	Northern Distributors Ltd. for £500 on account.
12th July	Paid petty cash postage stamps £4.
	Returned to Grocery Warehouse Ltd. faulty stock £43.
11th– 14th July	Cash sales £361 (banked)
14th July	Paid wages £33 (net).
	Paid by cheque insurance of £120 – year to 30th June 19. . .
15th July	Purchased goods for resale on credit T. Briggs & Co. £1,135.
	Credit Sale £79 Monkham Caterers Ltd.
15th– 21st July	Cash sales £623 (banked).
21st July	Paid wages £31 (net).
22nd July	Sale returned (faulty stock) of £8, from Welcome Caterers Ltd.
23rd July	Cashed cheque for petty cash £40.
	Paid petty cash sundry expenses £9.
24th July	Paid self by cheque as drawings £50.
	Paid petty cash, car expenses £23.
22nd– 25th July	Cash sales £490 (banked)
26th July	Credit purchase of printing and stationery from G. Norton Ltd. £23.
	Drew cheques for : Electricity £18.
	Gas £7.

9

A S

C

DR

Receipts

19..		Folio No.	Discount (Memo.)	Total bank	Sales	Ledger	Folio	
July 1	To Cheque			5,000 0 0		Capital a/c	12	5,000
	Cash sales			94 0 0	94 0 0			
2	Cash sales			102 0 0	102 0 0			
3	Cash sales			89 0 0	89 0 0			
10	Cash sales			730 0 0	730 0 0			
14	Cash sales			361 0 0	361 0 0			
21	Cash sales			623 0 0	623 0 0			
25	Cash sales			490 0 0	490 0 0			
31	Monkham Caterers Ltd.			60 0 0		Monkham Caterers Ltd.	4/16	60
	Welcome Caterers Ltd.	5/16	1 0 0	76 0 0		Welcome Caterers Ltd.	5/16	76
	Cash sales			613 0 0	613 0 0			
			1 0 0	8,238 0 0	3,102 0 0			5,136
			19		17			
				8,238 0 0				
Aug. 1	To Balance	B/D		327 0 0				

der

ɔk

CR

Payments

		Folio No.	Dis-count (Memo)	Total bank	Pur-chases	Wages	Ledger	Folio No.	
1	By Lease			600 0 0			Lease a/c	13	600 0 0
	Shop fittings			1,600 0 0			Shop fittings a/c	14	1,600 0 0
	Purchases			1,750 0 0	1,750 0 0				
	Rent			300 0 0			Rent a/c	30	300 0 0
	Petty cash			50 0 0			Petty cash	2	50 0 0
3	Rates			210 0 0			Rates a/c	29	210 0 0
7	Wages—net			28 0 0		28 0 0			
11	Grocery Warehouse Ltd.			1,000 0 0			Grocery Warehouse Ltd.	9/15	1,000 0 0
	Northern Distributors Ltd.			500 0 0			Northern Distributors Ltd.	10/15	500 0 0
14	Wages—net			33 0 0		33 0 0			
	Insurance			120 0 0			Insurance a/c	24	120 0 0
21	Wages—net			31 0 0		31 0 0			
23	Petty cash			40 0 0			Petty cash	2	40 0 0
24	Drawings			50 0 0			Drawings a/c	21	50 0 0
26	Electricity			18 0 0			Electricity a/c	22	18 0 0
	Gas			7 0 0			Gas	23	7 0 0
28	Wages—net			34 0 0		34 0 0			
31	Inland Revenue			9 0 0		9 0 0			
	Postmaster-General			6 0 0		6 0 0			
	Grocery Warehouse Ltd.	9/15	25 0 0	1,002 0 0			Grocery Warehouse Ltd.	9/15	1,002 0 0
	G. Norton Ltd.			23 0 0			G. Norton Ltd.	11/15	23 0 0
	T. Briggs & Co.			500 0 0			T. Briggs & Co.	8/15	500 0 0
			25 0 0	7,911 0 0	1,750 0 0	141 0 0			6,020 0 0
			20		27	32			
	Balance	C/D		327 0 0					
				8,238 0 0					

28th July	Paid wages £34 (net).
31st July	Drew cheques for :
	P.A.Y.E. £9.
	National Insurance stamps £6.
	Received cheques from :
	Monkham Caterers Ltd. for £60 on account.
	Welcome Caterers Ltd. for £76 (£1 discount allowed).
	Drew cheque in favour of Grocery Warehouse Ltd. for £1,002 (a discount of £25 being received).
26th–	
31st July	Cash sales £613 (banked).
31st July	Drew cheques in favour of :
	G. Norton Ltd. for £23.
	T. Briggs & Co. for £500 (on account).
	Closing stocks were :
	Packaging materials £25.
	Printing and stationery £12.
	Purchases £2,851

Show entries in books of account, extract trial balance and prepare Trading and Profit and Loss Account and Balance Sheet as at 31st July 19—.

Petty Cash Book

DR Receipts								Payments		CR
	Folio No.	Date		Voucher No.	Total	Packing materials	Postage and telephone	Sundry expenses	Car expenses	Nominal ledger
50 0 0	1	July 1	Cheque							
			Packaging materials		40 0 0	40 0 0				
20 0 0	17	3	Sales		15 0 0					Draw-ings a/c 21 15 0 0
		7	Drawings							
40 0 0	1	12	Stamps		4 0 0		4 0 0			
		23	Cheque							
			Sundry expenses		9 0 0			9 0 0		
		24	Car expenses		23 0 0				23 0 0	
		31	Balance	C/D	91 0 0	40 0 0	4 0 0	9 0 0	23 0 0	15 0 0
					19 0 0	25	26	31	18	
110 0 0					110 0 0					
19 0 0		Aug. 1	Balance	B/D						

Sales Day Book (including returns)

3

Date	Customer		Amount			Sales returns		
July 2	Welcome Caterers Ltd.	5	48	0	0			
11	Welcome Caterers Ltd.	5	37	0	0			
15	Monkham Caterers Ltd.	4	79	0	0			
22	Welcome Caterers Ltd.	5				8	0	0
			164	0	0	8	0	0
			16/17			16/17		

Sales Ledger

4   Monkham Caterers Ltd.

DR   CR

19..					19..					
July 15	To Goods	3	79	0	0	July 31	By Cheque	1	60	0	0
							Balance	C/D	19	0	0
			79	0	0				79	0	0
19..											
Aug. 1	To Balance	B/D	19	0	0						

5   Welcome Caterers Ltd.

19..						19..					
July 2	To Goods	3	48	0	0	July 22	By Returns	3	8	0	0
11	Goods	3	37	0	0	31	Cheque	1	76	0	0
							Discount	1	1	0	0
			85	0	0				85	0	0

Bought Day Book

6

Date		Folio No.	Total	Purchases	Printing and stationery		Nominal ledger
19.. July 1	Grocery Warehouse Ltd.	9	1,600 0 0	1,600 0 0			
	Northern Distributors Ltd.	10	670 0 0	670 0 0			
3	Grocery Warehouse Ltd.	9	470 0 0	470 0 0			
15	T. Briggs & Co.	8	1,135 0 0	1,135 0 0			
26	G. Norton Ltd.	11	23 0 0		23 0 0		
			3,898 0 0	3,875 0 0	23 0 0		
			15	27	28		

Bought Returns Day Book

7

Date		Folio No.	Total	Purchases			Nominal ledger
19.. July 12	Grocery Warehouse Ltd.	9	43 0 0	43 0 0			
			43 0 0	43 0 0			
			15	27			

Bought Ledger

8

T. Briggs & Co.

DR   CR

19..		Folio No.			19..		Folio No.		
July 31	To Cheque	1	500 0 0		July 15	By Goods	6	1,135 0 0	
	Balance	C/D	635 0 0						
			1,135 0 0					1,135 0 0	
					19.. Aug. 1	By Balance	B/D	635 0 0	

Bought Ledger (cont.)

9   Grocery Warehouse Ltd.

DR   CR

19..				19..			
July 11	To Cheque	1	1,000 0 0	July 1	By Goods	6	1,600 0 0
12	Goods	7	43 0 0	1	Goods	6	470 0 0
31	Cheque	1	1,002 0 0				
	Discount	1	25 0 0				
			2,070 0 0				2,070 0 0

10   Northern Distributors Ltd.

19..				19..			
July 11	To Cheque	1	500 0 0	July 1	By Goods	6	670 0 0
31	Balance	C/D	170 0 0				
			670 0 0				670 0 0
				19..			
				Aug 1	By Balance	B/D	170 0 0

11   G. Norton Ltd.

19..				19..			
July 31	To Cheque	1	23 0 0	July 16	By Goods	6	23 0 0

Nominal Ledger

12   Capital Account

				19..			
				July 1	By Cheque	1	5,000 0 0

13   Leasehold Premises Account

19..				19..			
July 1	To Cheque	1	600 0 0				

14   Shop Fittings Account

19..				19..			
July 1	To Cheque	1	1,600 0 0				

DR   CR

15   Bought Ledger Control Account

19..		Folio No.			19..		Folio No.	
July 31	To Returns	7	43 0 0		July 31	By Goods	6	3,898 0 0
	Cheque	1	1,000 0 0					
	Cheque	1	500 0 0					
	Cheque	1	1,002 0 0					
	Cheque	1	23 0 0					
	Cheque	1	500 0 0					
	Discount	1	25 0 0					
			3,093 0 0					

16   Sales Ledger Control Account

19..					19..			
July 31	To Goods	3	164 0 0		July 31	By Returns	3	8 0 0
						Cheque	1	60 0 0
						Cheque	1	76 0 0
						Discount	1	1 0 0
								145 0 0

17   Sales Account

19..					19..			
July 31	To Returns	3	8 0 0		July 31	By Cash sales	1	3,102 0 0
						Cash sales	2	20 0 0
						Credit sales	3	164 0 0
								3,286 0 0

18   Car Expenses Account

19..								
July 31	To Cash	2	23 0 0					

19   Discounts Allowable Account

19..								
July 31	To Cheque	1	1 0 0					

Nominal Ledger (cont.)

DR   CR

20 — Discounts Receivable Account

	Folio No.		19..		Folio No.	
			July 31	By Cheque	1	25 0 0

21 — Drawings Account

19..				
July 7	To Cash	2	15 0 0	
24	Cheque	1	50 0 0	
			65 0 0	

22 — Electricity Account

19..				
July 26	To Cheque	1	18 0 0	

23 — Gas Account

19..				
July 26	To Cheque	1	7 0 0	

24 — Insurance Account

19..				
July 14	To Cheque	1	120 0 0	

25 — Packing Materials Account

19..				
July 31	To Cash	2	40 0 0	

26 — Postage and Telephone Account

19..				
July 31	To Cash	2	4 0 0	

Nominal Ledger (cont.)

DR   CR

27   Purchases Accounts

19..		Folio No.		19..		Folio No.	
July 31	To Cheques	1	1,750 0 0	July 31	By Returns	7	43 0 0
	Purchase day book	6	3,875 0 0				
			5,625 0 0				

28   Printing and Stationery Account

19..							
July 31	To Purchase day book	6	23 0 0				

29   Rates Account

19..							
July 3	To Cheque	1	210 0 0				

30   Rent Account

19..							
July 1	To Cheque	1	300 0 0				

31   Sundry Expenses Account

19..							
July 31	To Cash	2	9 0 0				

32   Wages Account

19..							
July 31	To Cheques	1	141 0 0				

Trial Balance as at 31st July 19..

	Folio No.	DR			CR		
Capital	12				5,000	0	0
Leasehold premises	13	600	0	0			
Shop fittings	14	1,600	0	0			
Bought ledger balances	15				805	0	0
Sales ledger balances	16	19	0	0			
Sales	17				3,278	0	0
Car expenses	18	23	0	0			
Discounts allowable	19	1	0	0			
Discounts receivable	20				25	0	0
Drawings	21	65	0	0			
Electricity	22	18	0	0			
Gas	23	7	0	0			
Insurance	24	120	0	0			
Packaging materials	25	40	0	0			
Postage and telephone	26	4	0	0			
Purchases	27	5,582	0	0			
Printing and stationery	28	23	0	0			
Rates	29	210	0	0			
Rent	30	300	0	0			
Sundry expenses	31	9	0	0			
Wages	32	141	0	0			
Cash book		327	0	0			
Petty cash book		19	0	0			
		9,108	0	0	9,108	0	0

The balance as appearing in the sales and bought ledger control accounts have been used in the preparation of the trial balance and they are now reconciled with the actual bought and sales ledger accounts.

Debtors	£	s	d
Monkham Caterers Ltd.	19	0	0
Balance as per Sales Ledger Control Account	19	0	0

Creditors			
T. Briggs & Co.	635	0	0
Northern Distributors Ltd.	170	0	0
Balance as per Bought Ledger Control Account	805	0	0

The cash book reflects a cheque in favour of the Inland Revenue of £9 and one drawn in the name of the Postmaster General for £6, which have both been analysed to the wages column. The reason for these entries is that the true cost to a business of wages is the gross amount paid to employees out of which certain statutory deductions must be made for temporary retention by the proprietor as trustee on behalf of the Inland Revenue for P.A.Y.E. and graduated pension deductions, and on behalf of the Ministry of Social Security for National Insurance Stamps. The items for wages appearing in the cash book are the net amounts paid to the employees, to which must be added the remittances to the Inland Revenue and Ministry of Social Security to arrive at the gross cost for this expense.

The next stage in the solution is the preparation of the Trading and Profit and Loss Account and Balance Sheet which is principally compiled from the trial balance, but before this can be attempted a number of adjustments must first be computed.

The problem refers to the payment of rent on the 1st July of £300 in respect of the 3 months ending 30th September, to the payment of rates of £210 for the 3 months ending on the same date, and to the payment of insurance of £120 for the year to 30th June. A proportion of each of the three payments relates to a period in the future of the accounts, that is August and September in the case of rent and rates, and from August to the following 30th June in the case of insurance, and must be regarded as prepayments to the extent of:

	Profit and loss account, July			Prepayment Balance sheet (asset side)			.Total		
	£	s	d	£	s	d	£	s	d
Insurance	10	0	0	110	0	0	120	0	0
Rates	70	0	0	140	0	0	210	0	0
Rent	100	0	0	200	0	0	300	0	0
	180	0	0	450	0	0	630	0	0

Other adjustments are:

Depreciation of lease : Cost £600 with 10 years unexpired
    Depreciation   £60 per annum
                                 £5 per month

Depreciation of shop fittings : Cost £1,600
    Depreciation @ $7\frac{1}{2}$% per annum,
        straight line method   £120 per annum
                             £10 per month

Packaging material

	£	s	d	
Expenditure	40	0	0	
Less : Stock	25	0	0	Balance sheet (Asset)
	15	0	0	Profit and Loss Account, July

Printing and stationery

	£	s	d	
Expenditure	23	0	0	
Less : Stock	12	0	0	Balance sheet (Asset)
	11	0	0	Profit and Loss Account, July

Total stock : Balance sheet (Asset)

	£	s	d
Purchases	2,851	0	0
Packaging materials	25	0	0
Printing and stationery	12	0	0
	2,888	0	0

A Sole Trader

Trading and Profit and Loss Account for the Month of July 19 . .

	£ s d		£ s d
To Purchases	5,582 0 0	By Sales	3,278 0 0
Less : Closing stock	2,851 0 0		
Cost of goods sold	2,731 0 0		
Gross profit (16·7%) C/D	547 0 0		
	3,278 0 0		3,278 0 0
To Wages	141 0 0	By Gross profit B/D	547 0 0
Rent	100 0 0	Discounts receivable	25 0 0
Rates	70 0 0		
Electricity	18 0 0		
Gas	7 0 0		
Insurances	10 0 0		
Printing and stationery	11 0 0		
Packaging materials	15 0 0		
Car expenses	23 0 0		
Postage and telephone	4 0 0		
Discounts allowable	1 0 0		
Sundry expenses	9 0 0		
Depreciation :			
Leasehold premises	5 0 0		
Shop fittings	10 0 0		
	424 0 0		
Net profit for month	148 0 0		
	572 0 0		572 0 0

Balance Sheet as at 31st July 19..

Liabilities				Fixed Assets				
Capital account	5,000 0 0			Leasehold premises	600 0 0			
Add : Net profit	148 0 0			Less : Depreciation	5 0 0		595 0 0	
	5,148 0 0			Shop fittings	1,600 0 0			
Less : Drawings	65 0 0			Less : Depreciation	10 0 0		1,590 0 0	
	5,083 0 0						2,185 0 0	
Current Liabilities				Current Assets				
Sundry creditors	805 0 0			Stock as valued by the proprietor			2,888 0 0	
				Sundry debtors			19 0 0	
				Prepayments			450 0 0	
				Cash at bank			327 0 0	
				Cash in hand			19 0 0	
	5,888 0 0						5,888 0 0	

Closing Entries

The financial accounts have now been prepared, but before this exercise can be regarded as completed the procedure for closing the accounts in the nominal ledger (referred to under folios 12 to 32) must be mentioned for reasons that:

1 The sales and expenditure accounts in the nominal ledger will become confused with the transactions of the following financial period, and

2 The books of account as shown are not in agreement with the financial accounts due to the adjustments for depreciation, closing stocks, and prepayments which have yet to be recorded in the nominal ledger.

The various accounts in the nominal ledger as shown will be repeated to explain how they are closed off to facilitate the recording of entries during the following year without their becoming confused with those of the current year.

12   Nominal Ledger

DR   Capital Account   CR

19..				19..				
July 31	To Drawings	21	65 0 0	July 1	By Cheque	1	5,000 0 0	
	Balance	C/D	5,083 0 0	31	Net profit	✓	148 0 0	
			5,148 0 0				5,148 0 0	
				19..				
				Aug. 1	By Balance	B/D	5,083 0 0	

Nominal Ledger (cont.)

13   Leasehold Premises Account
DR   **CR**

Date	Particulars		Amount	Date	Particulars		Amount

19..
July 1
	To Cheque	1	600 0 0	19..
				July 31
					By Depreciation
					  P&L a/c
					  Balance
						√
						
						C/D
							
							5 0 0
							595 0 0

			600 0 0				600 0 0

Aug 1	To Balance :
	  Cost £600 0 0
	  Depn. £5 0 0
		B/D	595 0 0				

14   Shop Fittings Account

Date	Particulars		Amount	Date	Particulars		Amount

19..
July 1
	To Cheque	1	1,600 0 0	19..
				July 31
					By Depreciation
					  P&L a/c
					  Balance
						√
						
						C/D
							
							10 0 0
							1,590 0 0

			1,600 0 0				1,600 0 0

19..
Aug 1
	To Balance :
	  Cost £1,600 0 0
	  Depn. £10 0 0
		B/D	1,590 0 0				

15   Bought Ledger Control Account

Date	Particulars		Amount	Date	Particulars		Amount
19.. July 31	To Total Balance	 C/D	3,093 0 0 805 0 0	19.. July 31	By Total		3,898 0 0
			3,898 0 0				3,898 0 0
				19.. Aug 1	By Balance	B/D	805 0 0

16   Sales Ledger Control Account

Date	Particulars		Amount	Date	Particulars		Amount
19.. July 31	To Total		164 0 0	19.. July 31	By Total Balance	 C/D	145 0 0 19 0 0
			164 0 0				164 0 0
19.. Aug 1	To Balance	B/D	19 0 0				

16a (New Account)   Stock Account (Purchases)

Date	Particulars		Amount				
19.. Aug 1	To Closing stock	√	2,851 0 0				

Nominal Ledger (cont.)

17

DR					Sales Account			CR
19.. July 31	To Total Trading account	√	8 0 0 3,278 0 0	19.. July 31	By Total			3,286 0 0
			3,286 0 0					3,286 0 0

18   Car Expenses Account

19.. July 31	To Cash	2	23 0 0	19.. July 31	By Profit and loss account	√	23 0 0

19   Discounts Allowable Account

19.. July 31	To Cheque	1	1 0 0	19.. July 31	By Profit and loss account	√	1 0 0

20   Discounts Receivable Account

19.. July 31	To Profit and loss account	√	25 0 0	19.. July 31	By Cheque	1	25 0 0

21   Drawings Account

19.. July 31	To Total		65 0 0	19.. July 31	By Capital account	12	65 0 0

22   Electricity Account

19.. July 26	To Cheque	1	18 0 0	19.. July 31	By Profit and loss account	√	18 0 0

10

Nominal Ledger (cont.)

23   **CR**

DR   Gas Account

19.. July 26	To Cheque	1	7 0 0	19.. July 31	By Profit and loss account	√	7 0 0

24   Insurance Account

19.. July 14	To Cheque	1	120 0 0	19.. July 31	By Prepaid Profit and loss account	C/D √	110 0 0 10 0 0
			120 0 0				120 0 0
19.. Aug 1	To Balance	B/D	110 0 0				

25   Packing Materials Account

19.. July 31	To Cash	2	40 0 0	19.. July 31	By Stock Profit and loss account	C/D √	25 0 0 15 0 0
			40 0 0				40 0 0
19.. Aug 1	To Balance	B/D	25 0 0				

26   Postage and Telephone Account

19.. July 31	To Cash	2	4 0 0	19.. July 31	By Profit and loss account	√	4 0 0

27   Purchases Account

19.. July 31	To Total		5,625 0 0	19.. July 31	By Total Trading account	√	43 0 0 5,582 0 0
			5,625 0 0				5,625 0 0

Nominal Ledger (cont.)

28

DR				Printing and Stationery Account			CR
19.. July 31	To Purchases day book	6	23 0 0	19.. July 31	By Stock Profit and loss account	C/D √	12 0 0 11 0 0
			23 0 0				23 0 0
19.. Aug 1	To Balance	B/D	12 0 0				

29

				Rates Account			
19.. July 3	To Cheque	1	210 0 0	19.. July 31	By Prepaid Profit and loss account	C/D √	140 0 0 70 0 0
			210 0 0				210 0 0
19.. Aug 1	To Balance	B/D	140 0 0				

30

				Rent Account			
19.. July 1	To Cheque	1	300 0 0	19.. July 31	By Prepaid Profit and loss account	C/D √	200 0 0 100 0 0
			300 0 0				300 0 0
19.. Aug 1	Balance	B/D	200 0 0				

31

				Sundry Expenses Account			
19.. July 31	To Cash	2	9 0 0	19.. July 31	By Profit and loss account	√	9 0 0

32

				Wages Account			
19.. July 31	To Cheques	1	141 0 0	19.. July 31	By Profit and loss account	√	141 0 0

Opening Trial Balance as at 1st August 19..

	Folio No.	DR			CR		
Capital	12				5,083	0	0
Leasehold premises	13	595	0	0			
Shop fittings	14	1,590	0	0			
Bought ledger control	15				805	0	0
Sales ledger control	16	19	0	0			
Stock	16a	2,851	0	0			
Insurance	24	110	0	0			
Packing materials	25	25	0	0			
Printing and stationery	28	12	0	0			
Rates	29	140	0	0			
Rent	30	200	0	0			
Cash book		327	0	0			
Petty cash book		19	0	0			
		5,888	0	0	5,888	0	0

Partnership Accounts

To avoid duplication of the transactions as already explained, it is only necessary under the heading of partnership accounts to refer to the introduction of capital into the business, the division of profits between partners, interest charged on drawings and paid on capital and partners' salaries and the consequential entries in the partners' capital and current accounts, drawings accounts and the profit and loss (appropriation) account.

Green, Brown & Smith began to trade in partnership on 1st July 19.. under the business name of Green & Co. The partners contributed capital on the basis of Green £5,000, Brown £4,000 and Smith £3,000, and agreed to share profits in the ratio of 5:4:3, respectively. Drawings by the partners during the year were Green £400 on 1st October, Brown £600 on 1st January and Smith £800 on 1st April. The partnership agreement provides for interest to be allowed on capital at the rate of 5 per cent per annum, interest to be charged on drawings at 5 per cent per annum and prior to the annual division of profits Brown to be credited with £500 as partnership salary.

The net profit for the year ended 30th June 19.. was £3,460.

Prepare the cash book, ledger accounts and profit and loss (appropriation) account to deal with these entries.

1

DR

Green
Capital Account

CR

				19.. July 1	By Cash	13	5,000 0 0

2

Brown
Capital Account

				19.. July 1	By Cash	13	4,000 0 0

3

Smith
Capital Account

				19.. July 1	By Cash	13	3,000 0 0

4

Green
Current Account

19.. June 30	To Transfer Interest Balance	7 11 C/D	400 0 0 15 0 0 835 0 0	19.. June 30	By Interest on capital Share of profit	10 ✓	250 0 0 1,000 0 0
			1,250 0 0				1,250 0 0
				19.. July 1	By Balance	B/D	835 0 0

5

Brown
Current Account

19.. June 30	To Transfer Interest Balance	8 11 C/D	600 0 0 15 0 0 885 0 0	19.. June 30	By Interest on capital Salary Share of profit	10 12 ✓	200 0 0 500 0 0 800 0 0
			1,500 0 0				1,500 0 0
				19.. July 1	By Balance	B/D	885 0 0

6

DR   Smith
                              Current Account   **CR**

19.. June 30	To Transfer Interest	9 11	800 0 0 10 0 0	19.. June 30	By Interest on capital Share of profit Balance	10 √ C/D	150 0 0 600 0 0 60 0 0
			810 0 0				810 0 0
19.. July 1	To Balance	B/D	60 0 0				

7   Green
                            Drawings Account

19.. Oct 1	To Cash	13	400 0 0	19.. June 30	By Transfer	4	400 0 0

8   Brown
                            Drawings Account

19.. Jan 1	To Cash	13	600 0 0	19.. June 30	By Transfer	5	600 0 0

9   Smith
                            Drawings Account

19.. April 1	To Cash	13	800 0 0	19.. June 30	By Transfer	6	800 0 0

10   **Interest on Capital Account**

19.. June 30	To Green Brown Smith	4 5 6	250 0 0 200 0 0 150 0 0	19.. June 30	By Transfer to profit and loss (appro.) a/c	√	600 0 0
			600 0 0				600 0 0

11

DR				Interest on Drawings Account			CR	
19.. June 30	To Transfer to Profit and Loss (appro.) a/c	√	40 0 0	19.. June30	By Green Brown Smith	4 5 6	15 0 0 15 0 0 10 0 0	
			40 0 0				40 0 0	

12 Partner's Salary Account

19.. June 30	To Brown	5	500 0 0	19.. June30	By Profit and loss (appro.) a/c	√	500 0 0

Cash Book

13 (only showing appropriate items in bank columns)

19.. July 1	To Green Capital Brown Capital Smith Capital	1 2 3	5,000 0 0 4,000 0 0 3,000 0 0	19.. Oct. 1 19.. Jan. 1 April 1	By Green Drawings Brown Drawings Smith Drawings	7 8 9	400 0 0 600 0 0 800 0 0

Profit and Loss (Appropriation) Account
for the Year Ended 30th June 19..

To Interest on capital Partners' salary Division of profits : Green Brown Smith	600 0 0 500 0 0 1,000 0 0 800 0 0 600 0 0	By Net profit brought down Interest on drawings	3,460 0 0 40 0 0
	3,500 0 0		3,500 0 0

Balance sheet as at 30th June 19..
(Top left hand side only)

	£	s	d	£	s	d	£	s	d
Capital accounts									
Green				5,000	0	0			
Brown				4,000	0	0			
Smith				3,000	0	0	12,000	0	0
Current accounts									
Green Share of profit				1,000	0	0			
Interest on capital				250	0	0			
				1,250	0	0			
Less: Drawings	400	0	0						
Interest on drawings	15	0	0	415	0	0	835	0	0
Brown Share of profit				800	0	0			
Interest on capital				200	0	0			
Salary				500	0	0			
				1,500	0	0			
Less: Drawings	600	0	0						
Interest on drawings	15	0	0	615	0	0	885	0	0
Smith Share of profit				600	0	0			
Interest on capital				150	0	0			
				750	0	0			
Less: Drawings	800	0	0						
Interest on drawings	10	0	0	810	0	0	60	0	0
							13,660	0	0

Limited Companies

Many of the bookkeeping entries to be recorded on behalf of a limited company will follow the same pattern as those of a sole trader so far as concerns the transactions of a revenue and asset nature.

The transactions of a limited company not previously reported on will be those on the issue of shares and the preparation of the profit and loss (appropriation) account.

Peters Ltd., registered on the 1st July 19.. with a nominal capital of £20,000 consisting of 10,000 ordinary shares of £1 each and 10,000 $7\frac{1}{2}$ per cent preference shares of £1 each, issued on the said 1st July 19.., 5,000 ordinary shares and 5,000 $7\frac{1}{2}$ per cent preference shares payable as below:

On application, 10s 0d a share.
On allotment, 10s 0d a share.

The shares were applied for on the 1st July and allotted on the 8th July, and all cash resulting from the issue was received from subscribers.

On the following 30th June the profit and loss account reflected a trading profit of £5,500 out of which the following must be provided for:

1 The payment of an ordinary dividend at the rate of 10 per cent on the issued ordinary share capital as at the 30th June.
2 The payment of the preference dividend on the issued preference share capital as at 30th June.

(In both of the above cases, the adjustments necessary to provide for income tax on the distribution of profits is to be ignored.)

3 Corporation tax on the profits for the year is calculated to be £2,500.
4 A transfer to general reserve of £1,500 is to be made.
5 A capital profit of £750 arose during the year on the sale of a leasehold property.

Show the necessary entries in the books of the company and prepare the profit and loss (appropriation) account and the balance sheet so far as it is possible.

Peters Ltd.

DR				Cash Book			CR

(only appropriate entries shown in the bank column)

1

19..					19..		
July 1	To Cash :						
	Ordinary shares	2	2,500 0 0				
	7½% Preference shares	3	2,500 0 0				
8	Ordinary shares	2	2,500 0 0				
	7½% Preference shares	3	2,500 0 0				

Nominal Ledger

2

Ordinary Shares
Applications and Allotment Account

19.. July 8	To Transfer	4	5,000 0 0	19.. July 1 8	By Cash Cash	1 1	2,500 0 0 2,500 0 0
			5,000 0 0				5,000 0 0

3

7½% Preference Shares
Applications and Allotment Account

19.. July 8	To Transfer	5	5,000 0 0	19.. July 1 8	By Cash Cash	1 1	2,500 0 0 2,500 0 0
			5,000 0 0				5,000 0 0

4

Ordinary Share Capital Account

				19.. July 8	By Transfer	2	5,000 0 0

5

7½% Preference Share Capital Account

				19.. July 8	By Transfer	3	5,000 0 0

6

Ordinary Share Dividend Account

				19.. June30	By P&L (appro.) a/c	√	500 0 0

7

7½% Preference Share Dividend Account

				19.. June30	By P&L (appro.) a/c	√	375 0 0

Nominal Ledger (cont.)

8

DR					Corporation Tax			CR
				19.. June30	By P&L (appro.) a/c	√	2,500 0 0	

9

					General Reserve			
				19.. June30	By P&L (appro.) a/c	√	1,500 0 0	

10

					Capital Reserve			
				19.. June30	By Profit on sale of lease	NL	750 0 0	

Profit and Loss (Appropriation) Account

				19.. June30	By Balance	√	625 0 0	

Profit and Loss (Appropriation) Account
for the Year Ended 30th June 19..

			By Net profit	B/D	5,500 0 0
To Corporation tax based on these accounts	2,500 0 0				
General reserve	1,500 0 0				
Proposed dividend of 10% on ordinary shares	500 0 0				
Proposed dividend of $7\frac{1}{2}$% on preference shares	375 0 0				
Balance carried forward	625 0 0				
	5,500 0 0				5,500 0 0

Balance Sheet as at 30th June 19..
(Left hand side, only appropriate entries shown)

	£	s	d	£	s	d
Share capital *Authorized*						
10,000 7½% Preference shares of £1 each	10,000	0	0			
10,000 Ordinary shares of £1 each	10,000	0	0			
	£20,000	0	0			

Issued
  5,000 7½% Preference shares of
   £1 each, fully paid
	5,000	0	0			

5,000 Ordinary shares of £1 each, fully paid	5,000	0	0	10,000	0	0
Capital reserve				750	0	0
Revenue reserves						
General reserve	1,500	00	00			
Profit and loss (appropriation) account	625	0	0	2,125	0	0
				12,875	0	0
Provision for taxation				2,500	0	0
Current liabilities						
Proposed dividend : 7½% Preference shares	375	0	0			
Ordinary shares	500	0	0	875	0	0

CHAPTER 18

Insurances

If trading conditions become difficult, as they invariably do from time to time, there is, quite rightly, an inclination to prune expenditure as much as possible. One area which receives attention during a trade recession is insurance premiums, where it is a comparatively simple matter to reduce expenditure by the simple expedient of under-insuring, presumably on the assumption that 'it will not happen to me!' This policy has proved to be a disastrous mistake on numerous occasions, especially where the business damaged or totally destroyed represented the whole of the 'worldly goods' of the proprietor under circumstances invoking the application of an 'average' clause of an insurance policy. 'Average' is an insurance term to denote that the insured is standing part of the risk himself as, for example, stock valued at £2,000 being totally destroyed by fire but only insured for £1,000. The insurance company will only accept a claim for £500 in consideration of it being deemed that the insured personally accepted half the risk involved.

The principal policies are those of fire, loss of profits (otherwise known as consequential loss insurance), burglary, employers' liability, public liability and products liability. A fire insurance policy from a reputable underwriter will automatically also include the risks of storm, tempest, flood and explosion. An indication of a premium currently being demanded for this type of policy is 4s for every £100 of the sum insured unless there are exceptional risks involved, e.g. the storage of large quantities of inflammable materials, in which event a higher premium will be payable.

The purpose of a loss of profits policy is to provide compensation to meet predetermined fixed expenses arising from the happening of one of the insured risks, usually the same risks as referred to under the fire insurance policy. As an example, in the event of a fire causing partial damage to or total destruction of the shop area, no sales can be achieved and therefore no income earned. On the other hand, certain expenses such as rent and telephone must be met. A loss of profits policy will reimburse a proprietor with this expenditure which would otherwise have to be paid for out of personal savings or business capital. Also under this policy, but subject to the payment of an additional premium, it is possible to reclaim wages payable to shop assistants, thus permitting the continued employment of staff until the shop re-opens. The alternative to this course may otherwise be to dismiss the staff, with the unenviable task of advertising for and re-engaging assistants later when the shop has been repaired and redecorated. The premium for a loss of profits policy is approximately 5*s* per £100 of the total sum insured.

Another important insurance policy is one to provide against loss through burglary. Unfortunately insurance companies are finding that underwriting burglary insurance business is becoming more and more unremunerative and they are continually having to increase premiums while at the same time imposing increasingly more stringent conditions covering the installation of security systems which are expensive to buy or hire.

The remaining three policies mentioned are self-explanatory and they all include reimbursement of legal costs if a claimant should take legal proceedings. Employers' liability insurance is obligatory and provides for compensation to employees involved in an accident during the course of employment. Public liability insurance provides for compensation arising from injury to a member of the public while on the business premises and the purpose of a products liability insurance is to cover any claim from customers who have suffered loss arising from the use of products sold by the insured which cannot be held to be a fault of a manufacturer.

Many insurance companies offer a shops' 'all-in' comprehensive policy. Under such a policy the risks usually include those of fire, lightning, thunderbolt, subterranean fire, earthquake, explosion, burglary, housebreaking, storm, tempest, aircraft and other aerial devices, riot, strike, civil commotion, labour disturbances, flood, bursting and overflowing of water pipes, malicious persons, impact by road vehicles, public liability and employers' liability. The premium is approximately 10*s* per £100 of the total sum insured. The standard shops' 'all-in' policy will not cover the risks of consequential loss or products liability, but it is possible to enter into separate agreements to provide against the happening of these two contingencies.

Any reputable firm of insurance brokers will fully advise you, and fortunately this is one of the few services available to the public where no fee is demanded from them. Insurance brokers obtain their income in the form of commission from the insurance company to whom they introduce your business.

CHAPTER 19

Miscellany

In common with industry generally there are many statutory regulations affecting the retail trade. Some of the provisions can be very expensive to implement if a business is in any way deficient of them, especially those affecting business premises if they involve the erection of additional office space, fire escapes, toilet accommodation, washing facilities, etc.

The various Acts cover a wide field and hence it is intended to give only a precis of the more important sections of each Act, in addition to brief information on matters of general interest.

Contracts of Employment Act, 1963

The purpose of the Contracts of Employment Act, 1963 is primarily to afford to employees working in Great Britain (other than Northern Ireland) certain minimum rights as to conditions of service. It should be pointed out at the outset that the minimum rights are not effective in cases where an employee has separately negotiated terms which are an improvement in any respect on those as enacted. The Act also provides for regulations of a minor nature which are to the advantage of an employer.

The first sections of the Act deal with employers' and employees' rights to minimum periods of notice to terminate an employment and make provision for employers to give employees a written contract setting out the terms of employment.

There are exceptions to the foregoing and the important ones, so far as concerns minimum periods of notice, are that they do not apply to:

1 Part time employees who work or who are normally expected to work less than 21 hours a week.
2 Certain employees with fixed term contracts.

With regard to employees entitled to receive a written contract, the relevant exceptions are:

1 Employees already defined in (1) and (2) overleaf.
2 An employee who is the father, mother, husband, wife, son or daughter of the employer.

The minimum periods of notice which an employer must give to terminate the services of an employee are:

1 A minimum of 1 week's notice if the employee has been with him continuously for 26 weeks or more.
2 A minimum of at least 2 weeks' notice if the employee has been continuously with him for 2 years or more.
3 A minimum of 4 weeks' notice if the employee has been with him continuously for 5 years or more.

For the purpose of this calculation continuous service with a vendor or vendors immediately prior to the transfer of a business must be included.

An employee is only required under the Act to give his employer at least 1 week's notice if he has been with him or the vendor continuously for 26 weeks or more. Unlike the notice to be given to an employee, the period of notice of 1 week does not extend with longer service.

The Act does not prevent either the employer or employee from relinquishing their respective rights as to the period of notice if it is mutually agreed between them to do so, or if one of the parties accepts from the other a payment in lieu of notice. Nor does the Act affect the right of either party to terminate the contract without notice if the conduct of the other justifies such action, e.g. fraud, theft, perpetual bad time-keeping, etc. on the part of the employee, or grossly intolerant behaviour on the part of the employer.

With regard to the particulars to be expressed in writing, a contract setting out the terms of employment must be given to each employee not later than 13 weeks after the employment began. The written statement under the Act must provide for:

1 The name of the employer.
2 The name of the employee.
3 The date on which the employment commenced.
4 The scale or rate of remuneration or the method of calculating the remuneration.

11

5 The intervals at which the remuneration is to be paid, i.e. weekly, monthly, etc.

6 The hours of work.

7 Holidays and holiday pay, including any conditions relating to Bank Holidays or other customary holidays.

8 Incapacity for work due to sickness or injury, including provision for sick pay.

9 Arrangements as to pensions and pension schemes (if any).

10 The length of notice required to terminate the employment by either party, the minimum requirements of which have already been mentioned.

If there are any subsequent changes in the terms of employment, the employer must confirm them in writing to the employee within a month of the change becoming effective.

The Act also provides that it is sufficient for the contract to refer to any of the terms of employment to be in accordance with those as set out on notice boards or in registers to which employees have easy access. The practical application of this provision is in the case of a company with a large number of employees where it is not always possible to continually prepare individual newly written contracts setting out variations in the conditions of employment.

Both employer and employee have the right to refer any dispute arising from the implementation of the Act, or any question as to accuracy of the particulars required thereunder, to an industrial tribunal. The Department of Employment and Productivity will furnish full details as to how any reference to the tribunal should be made in addition to supplying the necessary forms.

D-Day

Monday, 15th February, 1971, is the selected day on which the United Kingdom will change over to decimal currency. The Pound Sterling will still remain the base unit but it will then equal 100 new pence. The symbol of new pence will be 'p'.

The decimalization of the currency will involve the minting of six new coins to consist of ½p (1·2d), 1p (2·4d), 2p (4·8d), 5p (1s 0d), 10p (2s 0d) and 50p (10s 0d). The first three coins, to be made from bronze, will not be circulated as legal tender until 15th February 1971, but the other coins, made from cupro-nickel, will form part of the currency before that date.

The physical change of the currency comprises only a part of the whole operation. Accounting and vending machines, cash registers and weighing scales will all have to reflect calculations in or accept the new coinage, and thought must be given to the problems as they may affect any particular business in good time. Many of the machines as listed can be converted. Therefore, there is no need to be stampeded into buying new equipment until you are fully satisfied that conversion is not possible.

With regard to the type of scale which also automatically calculates the cost of the goods as weighed, provided 15 days' prior notice is given to the local Inspector of Weights and Measures the price chart on the scale may be altered to reflect prices in terms of decimal currency.

Vending machines manufactured with slots to receive sixpences and half crowns will create special problems as under the new coinage no single coin will be provided for their respective amounts. However, several coin-receiving units are appearing on the market to accept a multiplicity of coins to equal a given value.

The Decimal Currency Board, of Standard House, 27 Northumberland Avenue, London, W.C.2., have recommended several books as additional reading to cover many aspects arising from decimalization of the currency and have also prepared a leaflet entitled *Decimal Facts* in which the following details are mentioned:

1 Clearing banks will be closed for normal public business from Thursday to Sunday, 11–14 February, 1971 inclusive, although restricted services will be available to ensure the safeguarding of cash and to meet the needs of travellers. On and from D-Day the banks will work wholly in decimals so that all cheques and other bank documents will have to be written in the £-new penny system and not £ s d.

2 Most Government departments will change over to decimal currency on D-Day, and our income tax, social security benefits and deductions will be decimalized. The Post Office and many shops and offices will also switch immediately.

3 A total overnight switch to decimal currency is, however, not practicable. It is impossible to convert or replace so quickly all the machines which now record £ s d amounts or operate with £ s d coins.

4 D-Day will be followed by a changeover period of not more than 18 months, during which machines will be converted or replaced and shops and offices will gradually make their own switch. For many purposes £ *s d* will remain in use during this period; pennies, threepenny bits and sixpences will not disappear immediately but they will cease to be legal tender at the end of the changeover period.

5 In the changeover period some of our shopping will be in decimal currency and some in £ *s d*: for a time we shall have to think in both currencies. This will not be as difficult as it seems, because both coinages are interchangeable from sixpence upwards.

6 To help shoppers before and during the changeover, many shops will mark items in both £ *s d* and decimal prices and conversion tables will be prominently displayed.

7 In the decimal system there is no exact equivalent of any sum that is not a multiple of sixpence. Official conversion tables will give recommended decimal equivalents: some penny amounts will be rounded up and others rounded down. If these tables are consistently applied there will be no overall increase in the cost of living as a result of decimalization.

8 There will be an intensive publicity campaign to prepare people for the changeover—through television, radio, newspaper advertising and posters. A booklet and conversion table will be issued to every household. Publicity material and teaching aids will be available to schools through local education authorities.

Income Tax

Sole Trader

As soon as possible after acquiring the business a sole trader should advise his local Inspector of Taxes of the fact, as it is necessary for him to be reclassified as self-employed, and as such he will be subject to the provisions under Schedule 'D' for income tax purposes. To expedite the transfer it will assist the Inland Revenue to advise them of the nature of the business, its address and the income tax reference number of the sole trader's previous employer. Under Schedule 'D' a sole trader is not liable to pay income tax on a weekly or other periodic basis as under the provisions of Schedule 'E' (P.A.Y.E.)

for employed persons, for the reason that his salary will not be known until the year end when the profit of the business is established. This is not to suggest that the total tax liability will vary between the two schedules, as a person earning £1,500 per annum in salaried employment will pay the same amount of tax as one earning £1,500 who is classed as self-employed, assuming, of course, the personal allowances of both parties are the same; the only difference is the method of collection. The privilege of being assessed under Schedule 'D' must not therefore be regarded as a tax free haven, and if a sole trader considers he is earning £30 per week, he should retain some of the profits in his business or personal bank account to meet the liability when it finally falls due. A sole trader should obtain an estimation of the probable tax liability from his accountant.

With regard to the wife of a sole trader if employed in the business, she will be regarded for income tax purposes as an employee and as such will be subject to tax under the P.A.Y.E. tables. If the wife was previously in other employment, the code number as shown on the P45 handed to her in duplicate on leaving her previous employer should be used, one copy of which must be completed and then forwarded to the Inland Revenue. Failing the wife having previous employment, a P46 should be completed and forwarded to the Inland Revenue who will grant a code number in accordance with the information supplied.

Partnership

The procedure established in respect of a sole trader will also apply to the partners of a business, who must individually follow the same routine. With regard to a wife, it must first be established whether she is a partner or an employee of the business and then acted upon accordingly.

Limited Company

A director of a limited company, whether or not one of its shareholders, is deemed for this purpose to be an employee of the company, and as such will pay income tax in accordance with P.A.Y.E. tax tables (Schedule 'E'). The code number to be applied will again be that shown on the P45. The salaries of directors should not be confused with the profit of the company, which is subject to corporation tax and payable once a year when computed.

National Insurance Contributions

From the male viewpoint, the distinction to be drawn between a sole trader, a partner and a director follows the pattern of whether he is a self-employed or an employed person. A sole trader and partner are self-employed persons and should contribute accordingly, whereas a director generally pays for a National Insurance stamp at the rate of an employed person, although provisions do exist under very special circumstances for a director to pay at the rate of a self-employed person.

The position is far more complicated so far as concerns a wife if she is engaged in the business affairs of her husband because:

1 If she is acting as an employee to her husband who is either a sole trader, partner or director, the wife may contribute towards a National Insurance stamp at the full woman's rate or at the married women's optional rate or, alternatively, make no contribution at all.

2 If she is acting as a co-director with her husband, the alternatives referred to in (1) above apply, together with a further option, namely, contributing as a self-employed person (woman's rate).

3 If she is in partnership with her husband, the wife may contribute as a self-employed person (woman's rate) or make no contribution at all.

The authority most competent to decide on the appropriate rate of National Insurance contribution applicable to a wife in these circumstances is the Ministry of Social Security, who will advise only after careful consideration of all the factors of the case.

Offices, Shops and Railway Premises Act, 1963

Disregarding all sections of the Act dealing with Railway premises as irrelevant to this book, the Act applies generally to all offices and shops (including catering establishments open to the public, wholesale establishments and fuel storage premises) in which people work. The Act also applies to such other areas of the premises used or occupied by employees out of necessity in carrying out the activities of the business, the purpose of which is to include within the Act the areas used as landings, passages, stairs, entrances and exits, halls, lifts, stairways, canteens and store rooms.

The inevitable relevant exceptions from the provisions of the Act are:

1 Premises where only self-employed persons work.
2 Businesses where the only people employed are relatives of the employer by being either a husband, wife, parent, grandparent, son, daughter, grandchild, brother or sister.
3 Outworkers' premises.
4 Premises where the total hours worked by all the employees does not normally exceed 21 hours each week.
5 Mobile offices.
6 Mobile shops.
7 Premises used for a temporary period only, the purpose of their use being accomplished within a short period commencing as from the date of occupation.

As a general rule the occupier of premises is responsible for complying with the provisions of the Act, but some responsibilities are transferred to the owner if the occupation is under a lease and if only for part of the premises.

The requirements of the Act are:

1 All premises, furniture, fittings and furnishings must be kept clean and no dirt or refuse must be allowed to accumulate. Floors and steps must be cleaned not less than once a week by washing, or if it is effective and suitable, by sweeping or by some other method.

2 A room used by employees to work must not be so overcrowded so as to cause risk of, or injury to, health. A room used by people for working in must be of such a size to permit 40 square feet of floor space for each employee habitually employed in the room or, where the ceiling is lower than 10 feet, 400 cubic feet for each such person. For the purpose of these measurements the areas of a room utilized by furniture, fittings and machinery etc. must be ignored. The space requirements just referred to do not apply to a shop area although this area will be subject to the general prohibition of unhealthy overcrowding.

3 With the exception of space used by the public, e.g. a shop area, provision must be made to maintain a reasonable temperature in rooms occupied by employees. A reasonable temperature for this purpose has been defined as 16 degrees Centigrade (60·8 degrees Fahrenheit) after the first hour. The heating system must not be such as to cause injurious or offensive fumes. A thermometer must be provided with easy access by employees on each floor if there is located on the floor a room falling within the temperature provisions. With regard to an area used by members of the public which is not included in the temperature provisions, employees must have access to heating apparatus and the opportunity of using it to warm themselves.

4 All workrooms must have effective and suitable means of ventilation.

5 Suitable and sufficient natural or artificial lighting must be provided in every part of the premises in which people work or otherwise use. Windows and skylights used for lighting must be kept clean and free from obstruction, unless whitewashed or otherwise shaded to reduce or eliminate heat or glare.

6 Sufficient toilet accommodation must be provided to allow at least one water or chemical closet for every 15 employees up to 30 employees, with a generally increasing employee-to-closet ratio thereafter, for which female and male staff must be counted separately unless:

> The number of people regularly employed does not exceed 5 at any one time—male or female—in which event only 1 closet need be available.

> The limitation of only 1 closet also applies where the regular employees normally work in the premises for only 2 hours a day or less.

> So far as concerns male employees working in premises with urinals equipped with means of flushing water, the number of closets to be provided must be in accordance with the following minimum scale:
>
> | 1 – 15 males | 1 closet |
> | 16 – 20 males | 1 closet if 1 urinal |
> | 21 – 30 males | 2 closets if 1 urinal |

with again a generally increasing employee-to-closet/urinal ratio thereafter.

The sanitary conveniences must be kept clean and appropriately maintained and ventilated and have adequate lighting. Although reference has been made to chemical closets, water closets must be provided wherever it is reasonably practicable to connect them to a drainage and water system.

7 Sufficient washing facilities must be provided for all employees. Sufficiency, for this purpose, is 1 washbasin where either:

a The number of people (male and female) working on the premises does not normally exceed 5 at any time, or
b Each of the regular employees (male and female) normally works in the premises for only 2 hours a day or less, and

in other cases, the number of washbasins to be separately provided for male and female employees must be as stated below, where it is reasonably practicable in the circumstances as affecting the premises:

1 – 15	1 washbasin
16 – 30	2 washbasins
31 – 50	3 washbasins
51 – 75	4 washbasins
76 – 100	5 washbasins
Over 100	5 washbasins plus 1 basin for every 25 employees or fraction thereof in excess of 100

The washing accommodation must be suitably marked in each case to denote its reserved use by a particular sex.

In premises (including shops) where more than 10 persons are regularly employed at a time and the washing facilities are also made available to members of the public, an additional washbasin for use by members of each sex must be made available in excess of the number required in accordance with the scale as already referred to for use by employees.

The Act also refers to premises with communal use of washing facilities by two or more employers, in which case the facilities must be sufficient in number to provide washbasins to comply with the total number of persons regularly employed in the premises.

12

8 An adequate supply of drinking water must be provided, and if not piped the water must be kept in suitable containers and changed daily. Drinking vessels must also be supplied, together with facilities to rinse them in clean water unless the vessels are disposable.

9 Suitable accommodation for clothing not worn during working hours must be provided.

10 A first-aid box or cupboard must also be provided, which must be readily accessible to and for the use of all employees.

11 Where persons employed in shops eat meals on the premises, suitable and sufficient facilities must be provided for them to do so.

With regard to fire precautions, the following general provisions must be followed in all premises:

1 There must be adequate means of escape in case of fire as may be necessary in the particular premises. In considering this question regard must be paid not only to the number of employees but also to the number of other persons (including customers in a shop) who may reasonably be expected to be on the premises at any one time.
2 While employees are on the premises exit doors must not be so locked that they cannot be immediately opened from the inside.
3 The contents of premises must be sited in a manner to afford free passageway to a means of escape in case of fire.
4 Properly maintained and appropriate firefighting equipment must be readily available for use.

It is illegal to employ persons in certain premises unless the means of escape have been inspected and certified as being satisfactory by the appropriate authority. The premises requiring such a certificate are:

1 Premises in which 20 persons or more are employed at any one time.
2 Premises where more than 10 persons are employed at any time other than on the ground floor.
3 Premises in the same building as other premises falling within (1) or (2) above.
4 Premises in the same building as other premises where indi-

vidually they may be excluded from the provisions of (1) and (2) above but when aggregated they do.

All premises falling within the definition of (1) to (4) above must take the following additional fire precautions:

1 All means of escape as specified in the fire certificate must be properly maintained and kept free from obstruction.
2 All fire exits specified in the fire certificate, other than exits in ordinary use, must be marked by a conspicuous notice to this effect.
3 The premises must have installed an effective fire alarm system capable of being operated without exposing anyone to undue risk. The alarm must be tested or examined at least once in every 3 months or whenever required by the appropriate authority. The system must also be audible or visible and must reach every part of the premises.
4 All employees must be made familiar with the means of escape and the routine to be followed in case of fire.

Race Relations Act, 1968: Employment

The Race Relations Act, 1968 relates to the whole field of social integration and it is, therefore, only necessary in this book to refer to those sections which deal with employment. The Race Relations Act, 1968 defines discrimination as treating a person less favourably than another on the grounds of colour, race, or ethnic or national origins.

The Act makes it unlawful for an employer or anyone concerned with the employment of others to discriminate against another person by refusing:

1 To employ him or by deliberately omitting to employ him for work which is available and for which he is qualified, or
2 To afford or offer the same terms and conditions of work which are available to others having the same qualifications, or
3 To afford or offer the same opportunity for training and promotion as is available to others having the same qualifications.

The Act lays great stress on the fact that it is unlawful to dismiss a person on grounds of discrimination.

There is a temporary exception from the provisions of the Act to employers employing 10 people or less until the 26th November 1970, after which date the Act will fully apply.

A further exception relates to vacancies which require attributes specially possessed by persons of a particular nationality. This provision is to counteract the now famous hypothetical example of a Chinese restaurant having to engage an Indian waiter against the wishes of the proprietor.

Another exception which is not limited in time is for the purpose of encouraging employers to have an integrated work force to preserve a racial balance. In accordance with these provisions, but only under certain circumstances, discrimination in good faith to secure or preserve a balance of different racial groups in a factory and office or a department thereof is permitted.

Of particular importance to businesses offering, usually for reward, to display advertisements on notice boards, it is unlawful to display any discriminatory advertisement or notice even if the subject matter of the advertisement is lawful.

Any proceedings arising under the Race Relations Act, 1968 are deemed civil and not criminal proceedings, with the Race Relations Board being the only competent authority for enforcement of the provisions of the Act. The Board may only do so in one of the designated County Courts (England), or Sheriff Court (Scotland) to whom they can apply for an injunction to stop future acts of discrimination and seek damages for actual loss and for loss of opportunity.

Shops Act, 1950 (as amended 1965)

In practical terms, the Shops Act, 1950 (as amended during 1965), is one of the most important Acts so far as concerns the average retailer, as it relates to permitted hours of opening of his shop premises. The main provisions are set out below.

Early Closing

Every shop, with the exceptions as referred to later, shall be closed for business not later than 1 p.m. on 1 weekday in every week. The weekday on which the shop is to close early for the serving of customers shall be, in general terms, the day as selected by the occupier.

The occupier of every shop to which the above applies shall:

1 Keep conspicuously displayed in his shop, in a position which is visible from the entrance or the outside of the shop, a notice stating the day selected as the early closing day.
2 The occupier has the right to alter the day so selected by specifying a different day in the notice referred to in (1) above:
a Provided 3 months have elapsed from the date on which the selected day became or last became the early closing day.
b Where in accordance with (1) above the occupier has altered the early closing day and a period of 1 month has not expired, the occupier may again specify the selected day for the early closing day of the shop. It should be noted, however, that where the occupier has exercised the right hereunder granted, he shall not be entitled to exercise the right again until a further period of 3 months has elapsed.

The main exceptions to the provisions concerning early closing are businesses for the retailing of:

1 Intoxicating liquors.
2 Refreshments.
3 Motor and cycle supplies and accessories to travellers.
4 Newspapers and periodicals.
5 Meat, fish, milk, cream, bread, confectionery, fruit, vegetables, flowers and other perishable articles.
6 Tobacco and smokers' requisites, and
7 Medicines and medical and surgical appliances.

General Closing Hours

Every shop is entitled to remain open late on 1 evening in every week until 9 p.m. in the evening and until 8 p.m. in the evening of every other day of the week. The Act lays down that the late day shall be the Saturday unless the local authority select an alternative day to be the late day, but the local authority has discretion to make the selection in such a way so as to fix different days for different classes of shops, or for different periods of the year or for different districts.

With regard to tobacconists, the local authority may select 10 p.m. for the late day and 9.30 p.m. on other days if two-thirds of the shops affected so desire. Sweet shops may remain open until 10 p.m. for the late day and 9.30 p.m. on other days.

To override the foregoing, the local authority may decide, with the approval of the Secretary of State, to fix hours at which shops in their area or in any part of their area must close. The order must not be before 7 p.m.

Sunday Trading

Every shop (with the exception of retailers of the Jewish Faith: see below) must close for the serving of customers on Sundays, except shops for the sale of:

1 Intoxicating liquors.
2 Meals and refreshments (but not including fried fish and chips purchased from a fried fish and chip shop).
3 Newly cooked provisions.
4 Sweets, chocolates and ice cream.
5 Flowers, fruit and vegetables.
6 Milk and cream (not tinned).
7 Medicines and medical and surgical appliances from premises registered under the Pharmacy and Poisons Act, 1933, or any person with a contract under the National Health Insurance Act, 1936, for the supply of drugs and appliances.
8 Motor or cycle supplies and accessories.
9 Tobacco and smokers' requisites.
10 Newspapers and magazines.
11 Photographs for passports.

This exception also applies to a funeral undertaking business and a post office.

Shopkeepers of Jewish Faith

Retailers of the Jewish religion may apply to the local authority to have their shop registered under the Act as such, and may accordingly open for business on Sundays, provided the shop is closed on Saturdays.

Subletting of Flats

A chapter has already been devoted to the question of leases as affecting business premises, in which no reference was made to the position of a proprietor with a vacant flat above the property not required for his own personal occupation. At the same time such a proprietor will no doubt be fully aware of the additional income the flat could produce if only a suitable tenant could be found on convenient terms.

It must be pointed out before any further consideration is given to the matter that, in the event of a proprietor wishing to sell his business at a later date, the value of his interest may be seriously reduced if, at the time of sale, the flat is occupied by a sitting tenant. If a proprietor is aware of, and accepts the risk then, subject to permission being granted under the terms of his own lease, he may proceed to find a tenant for the flat on the best terms he is able to obtain.

If a proprietor is not prepared to prejudice his price in the event of sale, but at the same time he would still like to earn additional income from the flat, he can consider the possibility of supplying adequate furniture, fixtures and a means for cooking, and letting the flat as furnished. As the law stands at present, if the agreement for a furnished letting provides for termination after the elapse of a specified period, then by giving the required notice vacant possession of the flat can be obtained and the business offered for sale to attract a better price accordingly. The solution of the problem by letting a flat as furnished has the disadvantage of involving the proprietor in expenditure for furniture, etc. which may be financially inconvenient to him if the money has been allocated for some other purpose.

An alternative method which may allow for the flat to be occupied without providing furniture and without involving a sitting tenant, is for its occupation by an employee, a manager, for example, if the agreement, preferably in writing, makes the position clear that the arrangement is a 'service' occupation.

A service letting is one where an employee occupies a property primarily in the interests of the employer for the better performance of the employee's duties: for the protection of the employer's property: for ensuring that the shop is open at all times during usual business hours: or as a general precaution against unexpected emergencies.

A service occupation must not be confused with a letting of a flat to an employee for no good reason other than to obtain rent as the employee may be able to establish a normal landlord/tenant relationship, and achieve sitting tenant status.

If a service tenancy is established and the employee finds other employment, he must vacate the flat on request of the proprietor—to be submitted immediately on cessation of employment—to enable the employer to find an alternative service tenant to continue with the safeguarding of his interests.

It should be noted on the sale of a business that if an employer wishes to offer vacant possession for the whole of the property it may mean dispensing with the services of the employee/tenant. Dismissing an employee to obtain vacant possession of a flat is an unpleasant duty, even in today's world of hiring and firing, and it is even more so if the person concerned has given good service. Thought can always be given, therefore, to allowing the position to remain unchanged in the hope that the purchaser will wish to continue with the arrangement, as service tenancies only affect the selling price of a business to a limited degree, if at all.

The happiest solution to the problem of a vacant flat, from the view point of a proprietor, is to apply for and obtain planning permission to change the user of the flat to that of office accommodation—a far more rewarding proposition. Unfortunately local authorities are reluctant to change user rights of residential dwellings in this manner because of the general housing shortage, and the chances of success of such an application are remote. Until recently a favourite ploy of many proprietors with a flat zoned as residential use was to occupy the flat for their own personal office use for a period of 4 years to establish office user, and then let the property as office accommodation without fear of retribution from any local authority. It is no longer possible to do this, as an established property user can only be permanently changed as a result of a successful application to a local authority planning committee.

Trade Descriptions Act, 1968

The Trade Descriptions Act, 1968 became operative on the 30th November 1968. The purpose of the Act is to protect the public from unjustifiable claims, outrageous or otherwise, concerning the history, quality, character, etc. of goods, and any violations thereunder will be criminal offences.

The Act states, 'Any person who in the course of a trade or business applies a false trade description to any goods, or supplies or offers to supply any goods to which a false trade description is applied shall be guilty of an offence.'

A trade description is defined as an indication, direct or indirect, and by whatever means given, of the following matters with respect to any goods or parts of goods:

1 Quantity, size or gauge.
2 Method of manufacture, production, processing or reconditioning.
3 Composition.
4 Fitness for purpose, strength, performance, behaviour or accuracy.
5 Any physical characteristics not included in the preceding paragraphs.
6 Testing by any person and the results thereof.
7 Approval by any person or conformity with a type approved by any person.
8 Place or date of manufacture, production, processing or reconditioning.
9 Person by whom manufactured, produced, processed or reconditioned.
10 Other history, including previous ownership or use.

A false trade description is, therefore, a claim made in respect of goods covering any one of the matters as listed in the foregoing paragraph, which effectively covers almost everything that can be claimed, and is untrue.

A trade description is applied to goods if a person fixes or annexes a mark or tag to, near or by the goods, or fixes or annexes a mark or tag in, on or with anything in which the goods are supplied. A trade description is also applied if:

1 A person places the goods in, on or with anything to which the trade description has been affixed or annexed, marked on or incorporated with, or places any such thing with the goods, or
2 Uses the trade description in any manner likely to be taken as referring to the goods.

A further case of when a trade description will be deemed to have been applied is if a customer orders goods specifying a particular requirement which a retailer fulfils under circumstances to reasonably imply that the requirement has been met. As an example, a customer asks for a size 72 × 60 inches woollen blanket and without comment the retailer places on the counter a woollen blanket measuring 72· × 54 inches which the customer accepts and pays for. Under the provisions of the Act, a trade description has been applied by the retailer and furthermore one which also amounts to a false description. All that was necessary on the part of the retailer to have remedied the position was for him to have informed the customer that he did not have a blanket measuring 72 × 60 inches in stock but he had one measuring 72 × 54 inches, leaving the customer to decide whether she still wishes to purchase the blanket in the light of this information.

Oral statements made by a retailer may also amount to the use of a trade description.

A false trade description is also prohibited under the Act in advertisements, irrespective of whether the goods subject of the advertisement are in existence at the time the advertisement is displayed. It has been common practice of some firms in the past to advertise goods before taking delivery of them, hoping that when the goods are finally received they will reasonably conform to the description of the goods as advertised. Conducting trade in this manner will no longer be tolerated under the Act in cases where the advertised description fails to match the true description of the goods.

Reference was made in Chapter 13 to sales campaigns and price reductions, and the following provisions are of particular importance in this respect. If any person offering to supply goods of any description gives, by whatever means, any false indication to the effect that the price at which the goods are offered:

1 Is equal to or less than a recommended price or the price at which the goods of the same description were previously offered by him, or

2 Is less than such a price by a specified amount,

he shall, subject to the provisions of the Act, be guilty of an offence. This means that the common practice of the prepared notice drawing attention to an unrepeatable, once-in-a-life-time reduction to 45s, when the price was only 37s 6d in the first place, must now be ruled out.

Continuing with sales periods and price cutting, the Act states that an indication that goods were previously offered at a higher price or at a particular price:

1 Shall be treated as an indication that they were so offered by the person giving the indication, unless it is expressly stated that

they were so offered by others and it is not expressed or implied that they were, or might have been, so offered also by that person; and

2 Shall be treated, unless the contrary is expressed, as an indication that they were so offered within the preceding 6 months for a continuous period of not less than 28 days.

This means that, if a retailer decides to have a sale by indicating price reductions, he may only do so without comment if the goods subject to the reductions have been on sale for a continuous period of at least 4 weeks during the previous 6 months at the price the retailer claims they have been reduced from. If a third party sold the goods previously at a higher price, or if the retailer has displayed them at the higher price for a period shorter than the period referred to, the public must be advised of this fact by an appropriate means.

It will be interesting to see how the foregoing paragraph is enforced. Arising from any prosecution under this section it may be possible to substantiate how long a retailer has stocked a particular item by reference to a date on an invoice, but how any infringement of the period of 4 consecutive weeks during the previous 6 months is to be proved is difficult to envisage, unless a retailer admits to the fact, or an army of officials is employed.

If a retailer refers to 'the recommended price', the expression must mean the price which is the recommended one of the manufacturer or producer for the retailing of the goods in the same area as the retailer. There have been occasions when a manufacturer has had a scale of recommended prices for different areas of the Country. It will no longer be possible for a retailer to select the highest recommended price for his own use if the highest price relates to another part of the Country.

Finally, with regard to services, it is an offence for any person, during the course of any trade or business, to:

1 Make a statement which he knows to be false; or

2 Recklessly make a statement which is false relating to any of the following:

a The provision in the course of trade or business of any facilities, services or accommodation;

b The nature of any facilities, services or accommodation provided in the course of any trade or business;

c The time at which, the manner in which or the persons by whom any facilities, services or accommodation are so provided;

d The examination, approval or evaluation by any person of any facilities, services or accommodation so provided; or

e The amenities or location of any accommodation so provided.

Trading Stamps Act, 1964

The main responsibility for conforming to the provisions of the Trading Stamps Act, 1964 is placed on the promoters of trading stamps; however, certain references are made in the Act to retailers who operate a stamp gift scheme.

Such a retailer must satisfy himself that all trading stamps issued by him show clearly on the stamp its value expressed in terms of Sterling.

Other relevant matters are:

1 Section 7(1)
   'In every shop in which a trading stamp scheme is operated:
   a There shall be kept posted a notice stating the cash value of the trading stamps issued under the scheme and giving such particulars as will enable customers readily to ascertain the number of trading stamps, if any, to which they are entitled on purchase, or other transaction.
   b A copy of any current catalogue shall be kept where it can be consulted by customers.'

2 Section 7(2)
   'That a notice required under section 7 shall be posted in such characters and in such a position as to be conveniently read by customers.'
   The notice as referred to is usually supplied free of charge by the trading stamp company.

3 All catalogues and stamp books supplied by a promoter and issued by a retailer must show the name and address of the former and, in the case of the catalogues, they must also show the current gifts available and the number of stamps needed in exchange for them.

4 The occupier or other controller of the shop may be liable on summary conviction to a fine not exceeding £20 by failing to comply with any requirement of the Act affecting him, as will any person who pulls down, injures or defaces any notice posted in pursuance of Section 7(2) referred to above.

Index